Trivial Pursuit™

THE AUTHORIZED GAME BOOK

CORGI

GUINNESS BOOKS

Design: Craig Dodd

© Guinness Superlatives Ltd and Horn Abbot International Limited 1987
Published in Great Britain by Guinness Superlatives Ltd,
33 London Road, Enfield, Middlesex and in paperback by Guinness
Superlatives Ltd in association with Corgi Books, a division of
Transworld Publishers Ltd, 61-63 Uxbridge Road, Ealing, London W5 5SA

Printed in Italy by New Interlitho S.P.A.

'Guinness' is a registered trade mark of Guinness Superlatives Ltd

Trivial Pursuit is a game and trademark owned and licensed
by Horn Abbot International Limited

British Library Cataloguing in Publication Data
Trivial pursuit, the authorized game book.
1. Questions and answers
793.73 AG195

ISBN 0–552–13332–9

HORN ABBOT
INTERNATIONAL

Contents

Introduction

Trivial Pursuit — the story

The Book — how to play

The Quizzes

The Answers

When the publishers of the world's best-selling book team up with the creators of the world's best-selling board game, you can be sure that something very special will result. And it has. **Trivial Pursuit – The Authorized Game Book** is here, brought to you by Guinness, publishers of genius.

Board games and trivia quizzes are nothing new, of course, but it took a spark of real inspiration to combine the two and come up with something of the appeal of Trivial Pursuit. The phenomenal popularity of the game all over the world is easy enough to explain. Everybody enjoys quizzes, but for most you need to be an expert on some obscure subject. Trivial Pursuit is different, because to be a Trivial Pursuit champion you don't. That's because Trivial Pursuit taps the human blotting-paper ability of people to soak up and store a vast collection of useless information. The other vital ingredients of the game are surprise – will the next question be impossible or easy? – and a degree of sadistic revelation as players

discover how much, or how little, their friends really know. There are no easy or impossible questions in Trivial Pursuit, just those you can answer and those you can't, and half the fun is in discovering how much you've known all the time without being aware of it.

In designing *The Authorized Game Book*, Guinness and Trivial Pursuit have kept all the characteristics of the original game, and added some more – including 500 illustrated questions which create a great new dimension of trivia material. What's more, *The Authorized Game Book* hasn't been created just to be browsed through, like the average quiz book. It's designed to be played competitively, like the game, by any number of participants up to 25, but *simply*, with no board, no tokens and no die. These are instructions for five different ways of playing *The Authorized Game Book*, so that you can enjoy it for a few minutes or a few hours, on your own or with friends. It's a whole new chapter in one of the greatest success stories of the past decade.

TRIVIAL PURSUIT – THE STORY

The story of Trivial Pursuit is a classic rags to riches tale about the birth of a brilliant idea and how it nearly didn't make it. It all started in a kitchen in Montreal in December 1979, just a few days before Christmas. At the table, playing one of the world's most successful board games, Scrabble, sat Chris Haney and Scott Abbott, both of them involved in the newspaper business and both with their heads crammed full of trivia. What, they wondered idly, would it take to create a game that would rival Scrabble in universal popularity and make both of them rich men? They say that it took them just 45 minutes to come up with the answer. It would have to be a game that tapped people's ability to absorb useless information. It would be a traditional board game, something less likely to date or go out of fashion than the new electronic games that were appearing on the market. And it would be a game that people could play socially, like a parlour game, instead of alone in front of a television screen. They even had a name for it. *Trivia Pursuit*. It didn't take long for

Chris Haney's wife to complete the whole scheme by inserting the missing *l* because, she said, it sounded better.

Most people, having come up with such an idea, would be content to leave it there – but not Chris Haney. He recruited his brother John to the cause and together the three partners formed Horn Abbot Ltd and set about turning the dream into reality. First they had to raise enough money to allow them to develop the game. After trawling the Montreal bars asking friends and strangers to invest in them, and being turned down by hundreds, 34 nervous venture capitalists were persuaded to part with a total of $40,000. In exchange they each received one share in the company. It was a shrewd move on their part, though at the time none of them realized quite how shrewd. At the last count those individual shares were worth $500,000 each.

With this money, and armed with reference books, the Haneys set off for Spain. Their destination was Nerja, and it was on the beach there that most of the questions for the Genus edition were written and the game perfected. They used the other people on the beach as guinea pigs for their ideas; if they laughed when they heard the answer to a question because, of course, they'd known it all along, the Haneys knew they'd got it right. They returned to Canada in 1981 with everything ready for the next stage — manufacturing and selling the first games.

It was at this point that it began to look as if the project might come unstuck. The technical problems of colour printing and collating the 1,000 cards needed for each game were so complex that they were held up for a long time. Even when they did find a way of doing it, it was expensive and pushed the price of the game up. Despite this they persevered, and by the end of the year the first 1,100 sets were ready for sale.

According to marketing wisdom, everything about them was wrong. For a start they cost too much — around $30, which was unheard of for a board game — and then there was no picture on the box showing what the contents were like. In fact the boxes had been deliberately designed to intrigue people, so that they had to buy one before they could find out what was inside. The critics were sceptical of this move and, they said, the questions were too difficult. The partners ignored the warnings and got down to the job of selling the first batch, touring the shops and drumming up sales themselves. It was hard work, but they sold all the games to the stores.

For a long while it looked as if the Jonahs had been right. Although the games were in the shops, they didn't seem to sell. The anticipated new orders didn't come pouring in. With their life savings invested, and after two years' work on the game, Abbott and the Haneys could only sit and sweat it out, hoping they weren't about to lose everything. For Chris Haney it proved too much. He collapsed under the pressure and had to be raced to hospital. Fortunately what had at first seemed to be a heart attack proved to be caused by stress, but nevertheless it took him weeks to recover — weeks during which the orders at last began to come in, more money was raised and thousands more games were produced. Against all the odds, Trivial Pursuit was on its way at last.

The next major move happened in September 1982, when a copy of Genus arrived in the offices of Selchow and Righter, the American company that produced and distributed Scrabble, the game which had inspired Haney and Abbott in the first place. The company president and the marketing vice-president tried the new game out and, despite the fact that they played it wrongly and couldn't answer the questions, found themselves instantly hooked. They signed it up.

The American marketing campaign that followed was almost as daring and uncompromising in its style as the game itself. There were no posters and no explanatory publicity. Instead, the image of mystery and exclusiveness that had surrounded the game from the start was continued. In one daring campaign, the country's top toy buyers received a series of intriguing little envelopes, each containing a sample question from the game and a few essential details about it, but nothing more. It was a gamble, but they were fascinated and bought the game, and their shops displayed it. Everything seemed ripe for success. Then, for the second time in its life, Trivial Pursuit wavered on the edge of disaster. Despite everyone's efforts, the public simply didn't buy it.

For the partners it was almost too much to take. While Genus was being launched on the American market, they'd been slaving away to consolidate their new-found Canadian popularity with the Silver Screen and Sport versions of the game. They were exhausted and dispirited. And then, just as it began to look as if the whole thing had backfired, news began to filter through that Trivial Pursuit had taken off in a big and quite unexpected way. The casts of the popular TV hospital drama series, *St Elsewhere*, and the film *The Big Chill* had discovered the game and were playing it on the set between takes. From there its reputation as a sophisticated and fashionable game grew, and with it sales, first in Hollywood and then throughout the country.

By 1984 it had become such an accepted part of American life that when a time capsule was buried it contained a copy of Genus alongside Michael Jackson's *Thriller* album. Journalists and writers from 21 countries were working on versions for their own markets. Personalities as diverse as Terry Wogan, President Reagan and the Royal Family were declaring their allegiance to it. And Chris and John Haney and Scott Abbott? They'd succeeded in their ambitions in a way that even they hadn't dreamed of. But given its origins and history, no one should have been surprised; everything about Trivial Pursuit was always unpredictable and unexpected.

THE BOOK – HOW TO PLAY

Half the joy of Trivial Pursuit is not just its teasing questions but its competitive game element – which is why we have created a number of games that you can play using *The Authorized Game Book*. You don't *have* to play them, of course. You can just browse through, testing your own knowledge, or you can use it as an ordinary quiz book. But if you do want to play, you'll find that unlike other quiz books you won't need a die or pencils or counters to keep score. *The Authorized Game Book* has been designed to be played anywhere, and at any time – in a car or on a journey, for an hour or just for ten minutes.

QUIZZES

The Authorized Game Book contains 120 quizzes divided into subjects which fall into six categories, coded:

G   Geography

E   Entertainment

H   History

AL   Art and Literature

SN   Science and Nature

SL   Sport and Leisure

THE GAMES

MASTER GAME

The Master Game can be played by up to 25 individuals. More players can participate by dividing into teams. To start, each player selects a playing number between 1 and 25. Players may choose any number they please, or a random system can be used, such as adding up the last four digits of their telephone numbers or their date of birth. If 25 bookmarks have been created, players may also find their playing number by drawing a bookmark at random from a pile placed face down. Players organize themselves so that they are seated in correct playing order, with the person with the lowest playing number on the right of the person with the next lowest number, and so on.

The player with the lowest playing number starts the game and takes either bookmark 1 or, if 25 bookmarks are being used, the marker which corresponds to their playing number.

Starting at Quiz 1, and continuing consecutively through the book, the player must attempt to answer the question that corresponds with their playing number in every quiz. Playing numbers cannot be changed during the game. The player proceeds through the book, answering questions, until they answer incorrectly. When this happens, they place their bookmark in the quiz at which they failed, and it is then the turn of the player with the next highest playing number to compete.

When all the players have taken a turn, the game continues with the first player. The book is opened at their marker, the page is turned to the quiz following that at which they failed, and the appropriate question is asked. The objective of each player is to finish the final quiz before the other competitors, and thus to win the game. Should a player fail to answer their final question correctly, on their next turn their opponents nominate a new playing number (one which is not being used by another player) for them to attempt.

For a quicker game, players can set a lower goal and aim to be the first to reach Quiz 50, for example. To avoid repetition, in subsequent games players adopt new playing numbers. They can also play the book in reverse, starting with the final quiz and moving backwards.

SHOWDOWN

Showdown is a revealing game in which players seek to prove their knowledge of their favourite category. Each player chooses the category in which they think they can do best. It doesn't matter if two or more players choose the same category. When each player has made their choice the others nominate an individual quiz within that category which they feel will catch the player out.

Players draw bookmarks, and the one who selects the lowest number starts at question 1 of their nominated quiz. If they answer correctly they attempt to answer question 2 – and so on, until they either complete the quiz in a single run or answer a question incorrectly. When this happens they insert their bookmark and the player with the next highest number takes over, starting at question 1 of their own quiz. The player who completes a whole quiz in the least number of attempts is the winner.

TEN IN A ROW

Open the book at any quiz and insert any bookmark. Players decide among themselves in which order they will play. The first player is asked question 1. If they answer correctly they proceed to the next quiz and tackle the next question 1, and so on. The object of the game is to answer 10 questions in a row. If they fail before they have answered ten questions, the second player starts at the original quiz, answering all the number 2 questions, as before. When all players have had a go, the first player starts again at the original quiz with the next question. If no one has scored ten in a row by the time question 25 has been reached the game can be continued by opening the book at random and playing over a new set of quizzes. Alternatively, the player who managed to answer most questions in a row can be declared the winner.

For a shorter game, substitute five in a row for ten.

OUTSIDE IN

A game for two players or two teams. One player starts at Quiz 1, the other at Quiz 120. The objective of each player is to be the first to reach the middle of the book by completing Quiz 60 (for the player starting from the front) or Quiz 61 (for the player starting from the back).

The participants agree who is to go first. The player's opponent then nominates the number of the question which the player is to attempt in their opening quiz. If the player answers successfully, they move to the next quiz, where the opponent nominates the number of the next question, and so on, until the player answers incorrectly, at which they insert a bookmark, exchange *The Authorized Game Book*, and the other player takes a turn. To win, a player must successfully answer a question in their final quiz and their opponent must continue to nominate playing numbers until they do so.

SOLO TRIVIA

Now a single player can enjoy Trivial Pursuit! For their first game, players start at Quiz 1, question 1. If they answer it correctly they continue to the next quiz and answer question 1 again, and they proceed in this way until they answer incorrectly. When this happens, they attempt to answer question 2 of the same quiz. If they answer correctly they continue to the next quiz and answer question 2 again; if they fail, they attempt question 3 of the quiz at which they originally failed – and so on.

The object of the game is to reach Quiz 120 on the lowest possible question number. If they do not reach the end, players can register how far they *do* get before failing at question 25. On subsequent games players can start with Quiz 120 and work backwards, begin with question 25 and work in reverse numerical order, or begin at any quiz and work their way through the book and back to where they began.

TEAM PLAY

Many of these games lend themselves well to team play, with teammates deciding how a question is to be answered. To avoid confusion, a captain should be elected to give the official team answer.

ANSWERS

The answers to all the questions in this book are contained in the separate answer section. The solutions to each quiz are listed in numerical order.

There are no rules to say how long a player may take to answer a question or how precise the answer must be – whether, for example, a last name is enough or both first and last names must be given. Players themselves decide these issues. Many answers include extra information and explanations, but players are not required to supply any information placed after the dash in the answers.

Should any player discover an ambiguity or inaccuracy in a question which the other players support, they should be considered to have answered the question correctly.

Trivial Pursuit™

The Quizzes

1. Which river basin constitutes one third of the European Soviet Union?

2. Which city can be viewed from the top of this landmark?

3. Which maritime country has the shortest coastline?

4. Which capital city lies at the junction of the Sava and Danube rivers?

5. Which Grand Duchy is bordered by Belgium, West Germany and France?

6. Which country is also known as the Helvetian Republic?

7. Which Italian port was connected to Rome by the Appian Way?

8. Which country boasts the southernmost point in continental Europe?

9. Which European city has the busiest port?

10. Which country does a true Bohemian live in?

11. What does the River Seine empty into?

12. Which is Ireland's main river?

13. Whose statue is this in London?

▽

(14) Which country was the victim of the Russian invasion of 1956?

(15) Which is the largest island in Europe?

(16) Which country do Serbs, Croats, Slovenians and Macedonians call home?

(17) Two countries are separated by the Gulf of Bothnia. One is Finland, what is the other?

(18) In which country is the Jutland Peninsula?

(19) Which is the farthest north?
a) Helsinki b) Oslo c) Stockholm

(20) Tyroleans come from two countries. One is Austria, what is the other?

(21) In which country did this airship crash in 1930?
▽

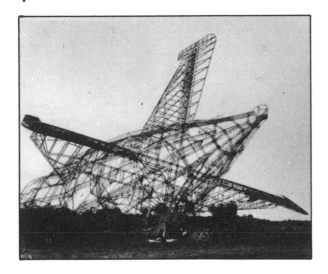

(22) Which is the largest country in Europe after the USSR?

△

(23) In which city are these New Year revellers dancing?

(24) On which body of water does the French resort of Biarritz lie?

(25) What present-day country would this character have called home?
▽

1. Which national hero was the subject of a Rossini opera?

2. Which English composer was most closely associated with the Aldeburgh festival?

3. Who composed 'Twinkle, Twinkle Little Star' at the tender age of five?

4. Which operatic heroine commits suicide on her father's sword?

5. Which 1967 song was based on the Bach cantata *Sleepers Awake*?

6. Which British pop singer played this composer in the 1975 movie about him?
▽

7. How many violin concertos did Beethoven write?

8. Where did Dvorak's ninth symphony come 'from'?

9. Which Mozart opera is a satire on Freemasonry?

10. Whose dream formed the subject of one of Elgar's greatest choral works?

11. What musical sign is this?

12. Did W.S. Gilbert write the words or music for such operettas as *The Pirates of Penzance*?

13. What is the connection between the composer Modest Mussorgsky and an 'exhibition' in 1874?

14. What nationality was the composer Borodin?

15. Which orchestral instrument is associated with Pablo Casals?

16. Which of Verdi's operas was based on the story of *The Lady of the Camellias*?

17. Who is conducting here?
▷

△

(18) What is the more common name for this composer's eighth symphony?

(19) For which English king is Handel said to have composed the *Water Music* as a peace offering?

(20) On the work of which English 16th-century composer did Ralph Vaughan Williams base one of his early orchestral pieces?

(21) What musical note is this?

(22) What is so special about John Cage's composition 4'33?

(23) Who achieved international fame with his ballet *The Three-Cornered Hat*?

(24) Which composer was the subject of the film *The Music Lovers*?

(25) Which German composer was the first person known to have written a concerto for only *one* of these instruments?
▽

1. What is the middle name of Britain's first female prime minister?

2. Which country did this 20th-century leader order his troops to invade in 1935?
   ▽

3. Whose name, apart from the astronauts', is on the Apollo 11 moon plaque?

4. What was the surname of Nicholas II, last czar of Russia?

5. What treaty did Hitler break in 1935?

6. What was erected overnight in August 1961?

7. How many stars did the American flag have in 1912?

8. Which group kidnapped and murdered Italian premier Aldo Moro?

9. Who was West German chancellor from 1949 to 1963?

10. Which ruler, traditional occupant of the Peacock Throne, was overthrown in 1979?

11. Which ship is referred to in this headline and picture?

The Daily Mirror

CERTIFIED CIRCULATION LARGER THAN ANY OTHER PICTURE PAPER IN THE WORLD

SATURDAY, MAY 8, 1915   16 PAGES   One Halfpenny

GIANT CUNARDER CROWDED WITH PASSENGERS CALLOUSLY SUNK WITHOUT WARNING OFF THE IRISH COAST.

(12) Where did Hitler's 1923 Beer Hall Putsch take place?

(13) How many times was Franklin Roosevelt elected president?

(14) Which French city was the centre of Marshal Petain's administration after the fall of France in 1940?

(15) Which king of Greece was deposed in 1973?

(16) In which country was this revolutionary leader executed in 1967?
▽

△

(22) What was this famous air ace's nickname?

(23) What happened in the North Atlantic on 14 April 1912?

(24) In which year were telephones first fitted experimentally into North American aircraft?

(25) Who is said to have 'invented' the 20th-century suntan?

(17) Of which country was King Zog head of state from 1928 until 1939?

(18) What happened in Argentinian political circles on 1 July 1974?

(19) Something special happened to the Archbishop of Krakow in 1978. What was it?

(20) Which British officer's autobiography is titled *The Seven Pillars of Wisdom*?

(21) In which southern European city were this husband and ▷ wife assassinated in 1914?

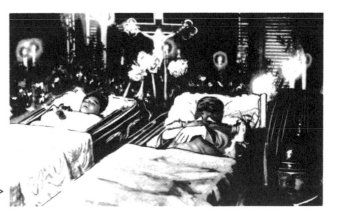

(1) What is the pseudonym of English spy novelist David John More Cornwell?

(2) What distinguishes the Perry Mason story *The Case of the Terrified Typist* from the others?

(3) Who created private detective Philip Marlowe?

(4) Who is the arch-enemy of Ernest Stavro Blofeld?

(5) Which literary character do you associate with this symbol?

(6) Who created Harry Lime?

(7) What make of lighter does James Bond light his ladies' cigarettes with?

(8) What famous name did Frederic Dannay and Manfred B. Lee write under?

(9) Whose cover is that of an employee of Universal Import and Export?

(10) What was this hero's real identity?

(11) Who created detective Mike Hammer?

(12) Which intelligence agency does Felix Leiter work for?

(13) Which detective lives on Punchbowl Hill and has eleven children?

(14) Which detective retired to become a beekeeper?

(15) What nationality was Hercule Poirot?

(16) Which author of many thrillers noted, 'The target of my books lies somewhere between the solar plexus and the thigh'?

(17) For which detective agency did Dashiell Hammett claim he worked before turning his hand to writing for a living?

(18) Who was 'our man Flint' in the movie?

(19) Who was Dorothy L. Sayers's aristocratic sleuth?

(20) Which Irish statesman wrote *The Riddle of the Sands*?

(21) Who was the author of *The Woman in White* and *The Moonstone*?

(22) What was the name of Sherlock Holmes's brother?

(23) Who was Karla's constant foe?

(24) This was the film made from the first Sam Spade novel. What was it called?

(25) Who turned down five proposals of marriage from Perry Mason?

1. What reptilian feature evolved into feathers?

2. What is the largest web-footed bird?

3. Which is the only bird to give us leather?

4. How many front toes does a parrot have?

5. What is the professional connection between this man and his two feathered companions?

▽

6. Which bird can swim but can't fly?

7. Which country has this bird as its symbol? ▷

8. Who was the artist who created the *Birds of America*?

9. What sort of bird will a cygnet grow to become?

10. Which actor led the Allied rescue party in the movie *Where Eagles Dare*?

11. What, according to the proverb, doesn't make a summer?

12. What is the most common domestic bird in the world?

13. Which type of bird has recorded the longest measured flight?

14. Which bird lays the largest egg in proportion to its own size?

15. What did one 'fly over' to win Jack Nicholson an Oscar?

16. Which famous Walt Disney cartoon character made a debut in *The Wise Little Hen*?

17. Which hotel did the *Eagles* sing about in 1977?

18. What sort of bird sat on the Cardinal Lord Archbishop of Rheims's chair, according to the poem?

19. Of which Australian state is the black swan the emblem?

△

(20) What was the nickname of this singer, who regretted nothing?

(21) What is a flight of geese called? ▷

(22) Who was the author of the story *The Snow Goose*?

(23) Of which continent was this bird originally a native?
▽

(24) What is the smallest bird in the world?

(25) How many blackbirds were baked in the nursery rhyme pie?

1 What was the first American stadium in which this man played?
▽

5 Which football team is known as the Canaries?

6 Which Argentinian footballer is the most highly valued player in the world?

7 Which national soccer team did Dino Zoff captain when he was 40?

8 For which Italian club did England's Mark Hateley first appear in 1984–85?

9 By what single name is this man, Artur Antunes Coimbra, known?
▽

2 Which South American country won its first World Cup soccer title in 1978, beating the Netherlands 3–1 in extra time?

3 What are the initials of the governing body of world soccer?

4 Which England player has scored the fastest goal in World Cup history?

10 Who is the only player to score a hat-trick in a World Cup final match?

11 Which country won the Olympic soccer competition in 1952, 1964 and 1968?

12 After whom was the first World Cup trophy named?

(13) In which year was the World Cup instituted?

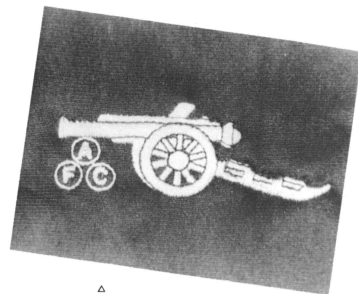

△

(21) Which club has this as its symbol?

(22) For which club did Jimmy McGrory play for most of his career?

(23) For which national side does Paolo Rossi play?

(24) Which is the most successful club in English League soccer?

(25) Which side won the gold medal in the 1984 Olympic soccer competition?

(14) Which club won the first five European Cup competitions?

(15) Which side did New Zealand beat 13–0 in 1981 to achieve the highest score in a World Cup match?

(16) For which Spanish club did Puskas and Di Stefano both play?

(17) Who is the most capped player in the history of Scottish soccer?

(18) When did Michel Platini become European Footballer of the Year for the second year in succession?

(19) Which city is the home of the world's largest soccer stadium?

(20) To whom is the Golden Boot awarded?

(1) Who sang *Anarchy in the UK* in December 1976?

(2) Who had a hit with *Delaware* in February 1960?

(3) In which 1940 movie did Katherine Hepburn star as Tracy Lord?

(4) Which 1951 MGM musical picked up five Oscars including best picture and best screenplay (for Alan Jay Lerner)?

(5) Where, according to an early Bee Gees hit, did the lights all go out?

(6) Where did Tom Jones's young puppeteer hail from in 1972?

(7) What film introduced the Gerard Kenny song *New York, New York*?

(8) Which group met their 'Waterloo' in 1974?

(9) In which American city would you expect to meet this family?
▽

(10) Which country didn't Evita want to cry for her?

(11) Where is this band going?
▽

(12) Who won the 1953 Oscar for best actress for her performance in *Roman Holiday*?

(13) In which North African movie is Charles Boyer supposed to have said, according to Hollywood legend, 'Come with me to the Casbah'?

(14) Where was the *Bridge Too Far*?

(15) Where did the first 'Road' film set off to in 1940?

(16) 'Tales' from where won Pier Paolo Pasolini first prize for best film at the 1972 Berlin Film festival?

(17) Where did David Niven, among others, spend 55 days?

(18) Which was the second James Bond movie?

(19) Where was the PTA Jeannie C. Riley was singing about in 1968?

(20) Where did the American werewolf find himself?

(21) Where was Alain Resnais's 1961 movie set 'last year'?

(22) Which American island lent its name to a 1979 Woody Allen movie?

(23) Where did the cast of the 1944 musical that featured songs like *Have Yourself a Merry Little Christmas* and *The Boy Next Door*, invite us to meet them?

(24) From which state did James Stewart come in the movie *Mr Smith Goes to Washington*?

(25) Who sang *As Time Goes By* in *Casablanca*? ▷

(1) What did Audrey Hepburn have at Tiffany's?

(2) Who was this, photographed with Joan Crawford, in 1931?

(3) Who was the pretty co-star of *Rebel Without A Cause*?

(4) Which sex symbol was decapitated in a car crash in 1967?

(5) Who played the part of a gun-slinging robot in *Future World*?

(6) What was Richard Burton referring to when he said, 'Apocalyptic — they would topple empires'?

(7) What was Bonnie's surname in *Bonnie and Clyde*?

(8) Who was Barbra Streisand's leading man in *Funny Girl*?

(9) Who was the first screen star to have a biopic made about his life?

(10) Which actor sent sales of undershirts plummeting when he took off his shirt in *It Happened One Night* and revealed that he wasn't wearing anything underneath?

(11) What were this star's last words?

(12) Who appeared with his wife Shakira in the 1975 movie *The Man Who Would Be King*?

(13) Who was the star of *The Kid*, who earned $2 million by the time he was ten years old?

(14) Which 1968 John Wayne movie earned him an Oscar?

(15) What 1960 movie finds Rod Taylor years ahead, trying to free people caught by the Morlocks?

(16) In which film was Dustin Hoffman seen approaching a swimming pool in a wetsuit?

21 How did Donald Sutherland's child die in *Don't Look Now*?

22 Which movie company produced *Mary Poppins*?

23 Which movie classic's recurring theme music was *Tara's Theme*?

17 In which soap opera is this actress currently appearing?

18 Who tied with Barbra Streisand for the Best Actress Oscar in 1968?

19 Whose first screen test notes stated, 'Can't act, can't sing. Slightly bald. Can dance a little'?

20 Which 'citizen' did this hopeful young actor become in 1941?

Continued from front page

24 In which play by Shakespeare is there a character who shares this star's name?

25 Which Dustin Hoffman movie took place in a Cornish village?

(4) What was the infamous pseudonym of the broadcaster Iva Toguri d'Aquino?

(5) Who said, 'When I'm good, I'm very, very good, but when I'm bad I'm better'?

(6) What does 'hell hath no fury like'?

(7) Who did Delilah betray to the Philistines?

(8) Which Irish activist became the youngest woman ever elected to the British Parliament in 1969?

(9) In the market place of which European city was this woman burnt at the stake?

(1) Who was the mother of this famous American family?

(2) What was Winston Churchill's wife's name?

(3) How much did this 'Star with the Million Dollar Legs' actually have her legs insured for?
a) $1 000 000   b) $1 250 000   c) $1 500 000

10. What kind of women gave Sigmund Freud erotic dreams?

11. Which famous first lady once observed, 'Woman is like a teabag – you can't tell how strong she is until you put her in hot water'?

12. What was the Princess of Wales's maiden name?

13. Which river is Pocahontas buried alongside?

14. What was the home of these famous sisters? ▷

15. Who was Good Queen Bess?

16. Whose wife was turned to a pillar of salt?

17. Which American wit commented, 'Brevity is the soul of lingerie'?

18. What was the surname of Emmeline, Sylvia and Christabel, founders of the movement commemorated here? ▷

19. Who was Napoleon Bonaparte's second wife?

20. Who was the first woman prime minister in the world?

21. Who married Lt. Philip Mountbatten on 20 November 1947?

22. Who asked Matilda to go a-waltzing?

23. Which woman has the most monuments erected to her?

24. Who was Svetlana Aliluyeva's father?

25. What was Marilyn Monroe's real name?

(1) How many nights are there in the Arabian nights?

(2) How many people took refuge in Noah's Ark?
▽

(3) What nationality was Aladdin?

(4) Who created the stories which feature this detective?
▽

(5) Porthos and Athos were two of *The Three Musketeers*. Who was the third?

(6) This star has a sister famous for novels such as *Hollywood Wives*. What is the sister's name?
▽

(7) Who wrote *Death in Venice*?

(8) What does the title of Hitler's *Mein Kampf* mean?

(9) Which Jean-Paul Sartre novel had a 'sick' title?

10. Who was Nikos Kazantzakis's most famous character?

11. Who is credited with writing the first detective story, *The Murders in the Rue Morgue*?

12. What is the last name of the brothers Dmitri, Ivan, Alyosha and Smerdyakov?

13. How many lines are there in a sonnet?

14. Who wrote *The Trial* and *The Castle*?

15. What nationality is the South American writer Pablo Neruda?

16. Who wrote the book on which this film was based? ▷

17. In which country were the great novels *Water Margin*, *Monkey* and *Dream of the Red Chamber* first read?

18. Which Alexander Solzhenitsyn novel was turned into a movie starring Tom Courtenay in the title role?

19. Who was the Canadian author who wrote *Literary Lapses*, *Nonsense Novels* and *Frenzied Fiction*?

20. What were Luigi Pirandello's six characters in search of?

21. To which university was this book given in 1943?

ENCYCLOPÆDIA 1768 BRITANNICA

22. What milestone in the history of literature was established by *The Gospel Book of Henry the Lion, Duke of* ▷ *Saxony* in 1983?

23. Which French writer filled 13 volumes with the contents of a single novel remembering the past?

24. What was Gulliver's first name?

25. Which Australian writer won the Nobel prize for Literature in 1973?

1. Which inventor said, 'Genius is one per cent inspiration and ninety-nine per cent perspiration'?

2. What glass-cleaning device did Mary Anderson invent in 1902?

3. What sort of machine is this?

▽

4. What does the acronym 'laser' stand for?

5. What is an Archimedes Screw used for?

6. Who is this famous engineer? ▷

7. Who was the inventor portrayed in the Walt Disney cartoon *Ben and Me*?

8. What did the machine called *Colossus* do in the last half of World War II?

9. Who invented the hovercraft in 1955?

10. Of which form of entertainment were these brothers leading lights?

▽

11. Which American city was home to the world's first telephone exchange in 1878?

12. Which household machine was first marketed under the name 'Thor' in Chicago in 1907?

13. What sort of machines were sold by 'our man in Havana'?

14. What sort of motor was invented by the Yugoslav scientist Nikola Tesla?

15. What sort of machine is this?   ▷

16. What did Sir Frank Whittle invent in 1937?

17. Which nursery rhyme was on the first gramophone record ever played?

18. What form of camera did Edwin Land invent?

19. Which motor manufacturer produced the world's first gas turbine car?

20. What does a seismograph measure?

21. For the invention of which medical machine was Willem Einthoven awarded a Nobel prize in 1924?

22. What does a cyclotron do?

23. What was the name of Dr Who's machine which   ▷ transported him through time and space?

24. How did a clepsydra keep time?

25. Which Renaissance artist first drew a 'battle engine', realized centuries later in the 20th-century tank?

1. What sport permits three minutes between chukkas to rest the ponies?

2. How many nail holes are there in a standard horse shoe?

3. What are the *irons* in horse racing?

4. How many furlongs are there in a mile-and-a-quarter racetrack?

5. What is the *near* side of a horse?

6. At which race meeting would you expect to see this sight?
▽

7. All thoroughbred horses in the world today are descended from at least one of how many great stallions imported into Britain in the 17th and 18th centuries?

8. Which American racetrack has the world's largest racecourse grandstand?

9. At which racecourse is the Prix de l'Arc de Triomphe raced?

10. Which historic race is held at Australia's Flemington Racecourse every year on the first Tuesday in November?

11. Where is the largest racecourse and racehorse training area in the world?

12. Who is the most successful jockey of all time?

13. Who is this on an unfamiliar steed?
▽

△

14 Who is this famous rider on *Princess*?

15 Which equestrian event is known in continental Europe as the *militaire*?

16 Which city is the home of the German international show jumping competition, famed for its demanding fences?

17 Which horse won the British Derby by a record ten lengths in 1981?

18 What is the name of the character played by Groucho Marx in *A Day At The Races*?

19 In which year were equestrian events first included in the modern series of Olympic Games?

20 In which Italian city is the historic Palio horse race run?

21 Which queen of England inaugurated the Royal Ascot race meeting?

22 In which British horse race did *Red Rum* make his name?

23 Which British Classic race is named after the Epsom home of the 12th Earl of Derby?

24 Which of the world's great races is run at Churchill Downs?

25 What is the correct name for this equestrian discipline?

▽

1. Which ocean liner burned and sank in Hong Kong harbour?

2. Which natural weather phenomenon kills more Americans than any other?

3. What extends more than 600 miles (960 km) from northwestern California to the Gulf of California with occasional earth-shattering consequences?

4. Where did two jumbo jets collide in 1977, killing 579 people?

5. Which city shook for 47 seconds on 18 April 1906?

6. What was the infamous feat of Germany's U-20 submarine?

7. What happened to the American nuclear submarine *Thresher* in 1963?

8. Which American city is reduced to rubble in the movie *Earthquake*?

9. Who plays the fire chief in the disaster movie *The Towering Inferno*?

10. To which present-day country does the island of Krakatoa, whose volcano erupted in August 1883, belong?

▽

△

11. What was the name of the airship involved in this historic disaster?

12. In which Indian city did the massacre featured at the end of the first half of the movie *Gandhi* take place?

13. In which year did this famous ship sink on her maiden voyage?
    a) 1912
    b) 1914
    c) 1919

▷

(14) Which East European capital was struck by an earthquake in March 1977?

(15) In which vehicle did this woman and her companions lose their lives?

▽

(21) In what city did a single terrorist outrage claim 243 lives in October 1983?

(22) In which famous yacht race were 23 boats either sunk or abandoned in August 1979?

(23) In which tunnel did a petrol tanker explosion claim the lives of an estimated 1100 victims in 1982?

(24) What creatures posed the threat in the movie *The Swarm*?

(25) In which American state did this volcano erupt?

▽

(16) Which scale is used to measure earthquakes?

(17) What was the name of the cyclone that devastated the Australian city of Darwin in 1974?

(18) Which Asian country lost approaching one third of its population in a famine in 1770?

(19) What form of disaster forms the theme for the movie *The China Syndrome*?

(20) What was the name of the settlement in Guyana where 913 members of the People's Temple cult committed mass suicide in November 1978?

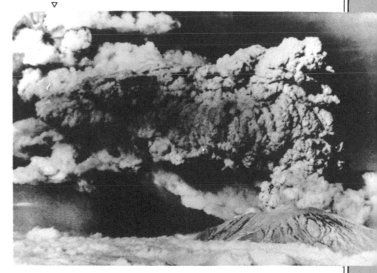

(1) What was Mickey Mouse's original name?

(2) What was the nickname of this famous trumpeter?

(3) Who is Leslie Hornby better known as?

(4) Who is called 'The King of Ragtime'?

(5) With what name did this star start life?

(6) Who was known as Mocha Dick?

(7) What was the secret identity of Don Diego de la Vega?

(8) What victim of the French Revolution was known as 'The Widow Capet' and 'The Baker's Wife'?

(9) What was this star's real first name?

△

(10) What was the name of this actress, known as the Divine Sarah?

(11) What was William Bonney better known as?

(12) Who was known as 'The Greatest Showman on Earth'?

(13) What was the nickname of William Joyce, World War II radio broadcaster?

(14) Which entertainer began his career under the name Silent Sam, the Dancing Midget?

(15) What was this actress's real name? ▽

(16) Which raunchy pop star started life as Annie Mae Bullock?

(17) What is Princess Aurora's better-known name?

(18) What is British actor Maurice Micklewhite better known as?

(19) Who did Lucille Le Sueur become after MGM ran a competition to find a new name for her?

(20) What was George VI's first name?

(21) Under what name did John Lydon achieve punk fame?

(22) What was the name of this man?
▽

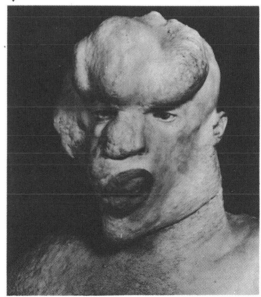

(23) Which actor became known as 'The Man of a Thousand Faces'?

(24) Who was born Marion Morrison?

(25) By what name is Richard Starkey better known?

1. Who replaced the assassinated Giacomo Matteotti in 1924?

2. To which war was this incident a prelude?
▽

3. What did America buy for $7.2 million in 1867?

4. Who succeeded this man as President of the United States?
▽

5. What is the supreme policy-making bureau of the Soviet Communist Party called?

6. Which organization was given the only Nobel Peace Prize awarded during World War I?

7. In which city was Bobby Kennedy assassinated?

8. What was signed aboard the *Missouri*?

9. How many years are there in a French president's term?

10. Which city was the site of the first meeting of the United Nations General Assembly?

11. Who succeeded Joseph Stalin as Russian premier?

12. How many American presidents were assassinated during this queen's reign?
▽

13. Which Israeli prime minister spent two years in a Russian concentration camp?

14. Which incident prompted the installation of the 'Hot Line'?

15. What was the predecessor to the Central Intelligence Agency called?

16. Which city did Kim Philby call home in 1964?

17. On which island did Napoleon die?

18. Which side won the Spanish Civil War, the Nationalists or the Republicans?

19. Which French statesman inspired and gave his name to this controversial Parisian building? ▷

20. In which country did the Gang of Four go on trial?

21. Which organization has its headquarters on New York's East River between 42nd and 48th streets?

22. Which conflict was known as 'The War to End Wars'?

23. Events in which country form the background to the film *The Killing Fields*?

24. What is the name of Mikhail Gorbachev's wife?

25. Whose mausoleum are these people queuing to enter? ▽

(1) What were the last names of Dr Henry . . . and Mr Edward . . . ?

(2) Who was this detective's landlady?
▽

(3) What army did Shaw's Major Barbara serve in?

(4) Who was H.G. Wells's least obvious title character?

(5) Who called his autobiography *I Am Not Spock*?

(6) What was El Cid's nationality?

(7) How many sons did Willie Loman have?

(8) Whose shoulder did Captain Flint sit on?

(9) Who was Lancelot's son in Arthurian legend?

(10) Which doctor was created by American Max Brand?

(11) What colour was Moby Dick?

(12) What was Lady Chatterley's first name?

(13) Who created Nicole in *Tender Is The Night*?

(14) Which novel centres on the romances of Ursula and Gudrun Brangwen?

(15) Who was Don Quixote's imaginary love?
▽

△

16. Which of this man's characters never appears in the well-known play that bears his name?

17. Who lost his 'precious' to a hobbit?

18. What kind of school did Pussy Galore run?

19. Who was Anastasia's and Drizella's stepsister?

20. Which Daniel Defoe character had everything done by Friday?

21. Which southern belle marries Charles Hamilton out of spite?

22. What is the secret identity of Vito Corleone?

23. What was the Great Gatsby's first name?

△

24. Who is the stern, high-minded village carpenter in the novel by this author that is named after him?

25. Whose finger is being touched by God in this famous painting by Michelangelo?

▽

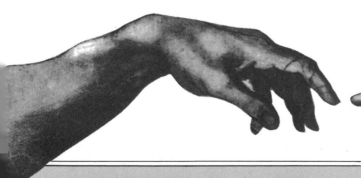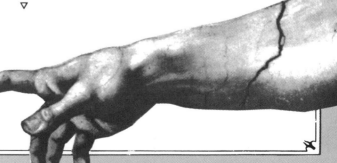

1. Before the introduction of the modern calendar, how long was a year to early inhabitants of Bali?

2. Which pre-Columbian American civilization believed that time revolved in cycles of 260 years?

3. Which Roman statesman abandoned the lunar month and took the solar year to be $365\frac{1}{4}$ days long?

4. Which artist is famous for watches like this?
   ▽

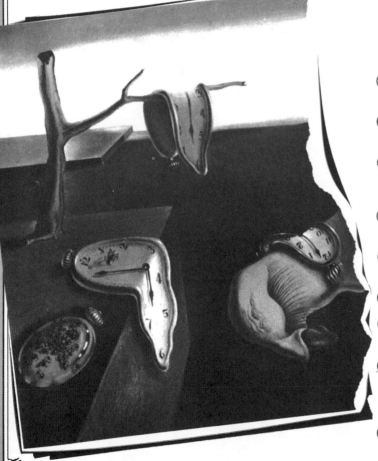

5. Which English king is said to have kept time by burning wax candles marked off in inches?

6. For which time keeping device is the inventor John Harrison particularly remembered?

7. Which atomic element has been used in recent years to construct clocks with an accuracy to within one second in 150 000 years?

8. Were days longer, shorter, or the same length when life began on earth compared with their length today?

9. Which line of Meridian does the International Date Line follow in the main?

10. 'Time and . . .' what 'wait for no man'?

11. What hour did the clock strike causing the mouse in the nursery rhyme to fall down?

12. What date followed 2 September in 1752, when Great Britain and the American colonies adopted the Gregorian calendar?
    a) 3 September   b) 9 September   c) 14 September

13. In which century was the first watch invented?

△

(14) Name one of the two months covered by this sign of the zodiac.

(15) How many time zones is the world divided into?

(16) How many bells are rung at sea to bring in the New Year?

(17) Who starred as the commanding officer who finally cracks up in the 1949 movie *Twelve O'Clock High*?

(18) How long is 10^2 seconds?

(19) What is the popular name of this clock?

▽

(20) How many months were there in the earliest Roman calendars?

(21) What instrument did navigators use before the advent of the quadrant to give longitude and time of day at sea?

(22) Using this information, and assuming standard time differences, can you work out what hour it is in New York?

▽

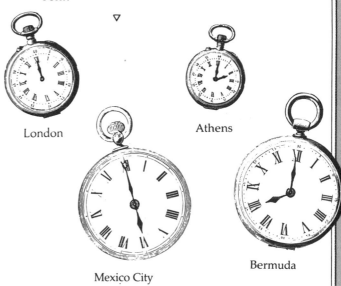

London

Athens

Mexico City

Bermuda

(23) What important historical application does radioactive carbon-14 offer?

(24) Which European capital is home to the world's most accurate mechanical clock?

(25) Which English cathedral has the oldest surviving working clock in the world?

1 The waters of which ocean wash against Copacobana Beach?

2 Where would you be holidaying if you visited this church, which later became a mosque?

3 To which European country would you need to travel to spend a vacation in the Engadine?

4 Which country is home to the original Spa?

5 In which city would you need to stay if you wanted to visit the world's largest hotel (measured by number of rooms)?

6 Which Canadian province boasts the Dinosaur Park at Drumheller?

7 To which country would you be heading if you were flying with the Varig airline to its home base?

8 Which popular vacation island is served by Grantley Adams airport?

9 In which country would you be if you visited this building?

△

(10) What is the name of the Wyoming park in which this geyser faithfully performs?

(11) Which British pop singer revelled in a *Summer Holiday* in 1962?

(12) Which international governing body is concerned with airline traffic?

(13) Which American state is the home of EPCOT?

(14) Which area of France is home to the original fish stew, or soup, known as *bouillabaisse*?

(15) From what does Paris's famed *Place de Vosges* take its name?

(16) Which tropical holiday paradise lies 400 miles (640 km) south-west of Sri Lanka?

(17) What form of holiday takes its name from a Swahili word that originated from the Arabic for 'journey'?

(18) Which Indian Ocean holiday destination did Albert Réné take control of in a coup in June 1977?

(19) What is the native language spoken in the Algarve?

(20) Which notable carnival was the destination in *Easy Rider*?

(21) In which famous 'Côte' are Antibes, Cannes, Juan-les-Pins and Nice?

(22) Who wrote *California Suite*?

(23) In which African hotel was Princess Elizabeth staying in February 1952 when news of her father's death made her Queen?

(24) Which Italian town is nicknamed The Manhattan of Tuscany because of its famous towers?

(25) In which country would you be if you visited this island?

▽

(1) What is the name of the Antarctic base established by Richard Byrd?

(2) Which country's flag was this man sailing under when he made the discovery for which he is best remembered?

▽

(3) What was the *Mayflower's* last port of call before setting sail for America?

(4) Who used this method of transport to reach the South Pole in December 1911?

▽

(5) Who is considered to be the patron saint of travellers?

(6) What nationality was Sven Hedin, the explorer of Central Asia at the turn of the century?

(7) Which English explorer was set adrift by his mutinous crew near the bay that bears his name?

(8) Which famous Italian explorer is buried in the Dominican Republic?

(9) Who gave his name to one of the continental landmasses?

(10) Who went for a short walk in the Hindu Kush?

(11) Who discovered the sea route to India via the Cape of Good Hope?

(12) Who led the British Trans-Globe expedition?

(13) Which 17th-century explorer was buried with a pipe and a box of tobacco?

▷

△

14 What is the name of the Irish monk believed to have led a party that sailed to America in a leather boat?

15 Who was emperor of China when Marco Polo visited his court?

▷

16 Which Chinese explorer led seven diplomatic expeditions for the Ming dynasty early in the 15th century?

17 Which European sailor led the first expedition to the St Lawrence river?

18 Who did John Hanning Speke accompany on the 1857 expedition to find the great lakes of equatorial Africa?

19 Which ship carried Charles Darwin to the Pacific in the early 1830s?

20 Which of the world's great deserts did Réné Caillié cross between 1827 and 1828?

21 With which African river is Mungo Park most closely associated?

22 What is this famous Antarctic explorer's middle name?

▽

23 What were Baffin, Frobisher and Franklin all searching for?

24 On which of Captain Cook's voyages did he discover Antarctica?

25 Which nation established a trading settlement at Cape Town in 1652?

1. Which rock and roll star caused a 1958 scandal by marrying his thirteen-year-old cousin?

2. Who swapped this man for Mick Jagger?
   ▽

3. With whom, according to the gossip columns, did Kim Novak have a scandalous 1957 romance?

4. Who did this actress leave her first husband for? ▷

5. What year did Marilyn Monroe die?

6. What word, meaning 'the exploitation of slum tenants' was coined after this man's exposure in 1963?
   ▽

7. Which singer paid a ransom of $240 000 to free his kidnapped son?

8. Why did this star have to hand back her Miss Hungary 1936 crown?
   ▽

9. Who did Elizabeth Taylor divorce ten days before she married Richard Burton?

10. In which film did Bette Davis cause a scandal by wearing a daring red gown to a society ball?

11. Who was Natalie Wood married to when she died?

12. Why was Wing-Commander Peter Townsend prevented from marrying Princess Margaret in 1956?

13. Which former UN secretary-general and Austrian president was accused of links with the Nazis?

14. Which singer said, 'First I lost my weight. Then I lost my voice. Now I've lost Onassis'?

15. Who did Marilyn Barnett sue under the 'palimony' laws in 1981, after a lesbian affair?

16. Who, 'starkers', made Andy randy?

17. Who was Mrs Simpson's first husband?

18. What was the nickname of this American president's wife?
▽

19. Which band made *Rumours*, the best selling album of 1977?

20. Which princess's last words were reputedly, 'I want you to believe I was driving'?

21. Which descendant of the Prophet Muhāmmād married this film star?
▽

22. Which Hollywood star was Erin Fleming accused of mistreating?

23. Which English cricketer bowled himself out of the game after coming clean about his drug-taking?

24. Which of 'Tricky Dicky's' right-hand men spiralled out of office in 1973 after putting his hand in the wrong pocket?

25. Which British royal discovered a Nazi skeleton in her family's cupboard in 1985?

(1) Who did Peeping Tom peep at?

(2) Where was King Arthur's Court?

(3) Which gate does the three-headed dog Cerberus guard?

(4) In which of the *Mad Max* movies did this leader of Bartertown appear?
▽

(5) Who flew too near the sun wearing wings made with wax?
▽

(6) Who made a boat out of gopher wood?

(7) What do you need to kiss to be endowed with great powers of persuasion?

(8) Who saw this sight in the heavens and took it as a sign that 'a kingdom wanted a king'?
▽

(9) Which side of the bed does superstition say is the 'wrong' side?

(10) Who is this mythical figure?
▷

11. Who, with his twin Romulus, was suckled by a wolf?

12. What in 1975 did 18 Nobel laureates claim has no basis in fact?

13. Which day of the week is named after the Norse Goddess of Love, wife of Odin?

14. Who was the legendary commander of the Greek armies at the siege of Troy?

15. Who is still holding up the sky according to ancient legends?

16. Which 20th-century English play takes its title from a legendary king of Cyprus who fell in love with a statue?

17. What was the resting place of Scandinavian warriors killed in battle called?

18. Whose words of wisdom drew visitors to this ancient site in Greece?
▽

19. What was the name of the group of oarsmen Jason commanded on his famous voyage in search of the Golden Fleece?

20. On which book did Lerner and Loewe base their stage musical of the Arthurian myth?

21. Which forest was home to Robin Hood?

△

22. What is the name of this mythical creature?

23. Who was the composer of *Orpheus in the Underworld*?

24. Where was Quasimodo the bellringer?

25. Which famous tap-dancer, who doesn't mind wet weather, went to Xanadu in 1980?

△

(1) Which French painter designed this dress?

(2) Which artist was the first to develop this style of painting?

▽

(3) Which Australian painter counts *Themes From the Career of Ned Kelly* among his works?

(4) What was Utrillo's first name?

(5) Who was this famous artist's well known artist sister?

▽

(6) What style of art did Al Capp call 'a product of the untalented, sold by the unprincipled to the utterly bewildered'?

(7) Who painted *Campbell's Soupcans*?

(8) What single exclamation is the title for Roy Lichtenstein's painting with its giant strip-cartoon dog-fight theme?

(9) What nationality was the painter Diego Rivera?

(10) Which French impressionist was famous for his paintings of ballet dancers?

11) Who was artist Pietro Anigoni's most famous subject?

△

12) Who is this famous sculptress?

13) Which Spanish artist promised to eat his wife after her death?

14) The life of which artist was Somerset Maugham's *The Moon and Sixpence* based on?

15) Which country did Rene Magritte call home?

16) Which artist was most famous for his posters of Paris?

17) Which two French impressionist artists had the same name but for one letter?

18) Which painter's works include *Sunflowers* and *Starry Night*?

19) What is the more common name given to the art form known in German as *Jugendstil*?

20) Which modern British painter designed a set for a Glyndebourne Opera production of *The Magic Flute*?

21) Which artistic movement was greatly influenced by Freud's theories of psychoanalysis?

△

22) To which 'school' of art does this painting belong?

23) Which member of the New York School is regarded as the chief American exponent of Action Painting?

24) Which European artist described his work as 'taking a line for a walk'?

25) Which artistic movement began in Zurich during the First World War and took its name from the French for 'hobby-horse'?

(1) Which season is hail most prevalent in?

(2) What yellow, fossilized resin did the Greeks and Romans use in jewellery?

(3) Which global conservation organization does this ship ▷ belong to?

(4) What is the world's most common compound?

(5) Coal and oil are two important fossil fuels, but what is the third?

(6) How many colours are there in a rainbow?

(7) Which pole gets more sunlight, the North Pole or the South Pole?

(8) What rings the globe $23\frac{1}{2}°$ south of the North Pole?

(9) What is the term for this kind of hanging limestone deposit?
▽

△

21. Which character, created by David Bowie, sings, 'Planet Earth is blue/And there's nothing I can do'?

22. Which of the Earth's poles tilts towards the sun between 21 June and 21 September?

23. Who first described the world as a 'global village'?

24. What makes up 3.5 per cent of the oceans?

25. What planetary connections does this man have?
▽

10. Which spacecraft, launched in 1972, carried this guide to planet Earth?

11. What is the term for the outward flow of water following high tide?

12. What fraction of an iceberg shows above water?

13. What direction is the Sahara expanding in by half a mile a year?

14. What is the study of fossils called?

15. When are shadows shorter — in summer or winter?

16. What is the most common colour of amethyst?

17. What is permanently frozen sub-soil called?

18. What are 'The Star of Africa' and 'Cullinan II'?

19. What percentage of the Earth's water is drinkable?

20. What year followed 1 BC?

1. Which black American runner, crippled as a child, struck gold at the 1960 Olympics?

2. In which track and field event did this Tarzan win a silver medal at the 1928 Summer Olympics?

▽

3. By what name is the hop, step and jump now known?

4. Which British runner won the men's 100 m at the 1924 Olympics?

5. In which event did Tiina Lillak become Finland's first ever track and field record holder?

6. How many events are there in a heptathlon?

7. In which year were female athletes first given a 'sex test' at the Olympic Games?

8. What is the name of this British athlete, who set world records for the men's 1500 m and mile within two weeks of each other in July 1985? ▷

9. What is the first instruction given to runners by the starter of a race?

10. Who is the only athlete to have set six world records in one day?

11. Which famous Australian record-holding athlete carried the Olympic torch into the stadium at the 1956 games in Melbourne?

12. Of which Olympic Games did Leni Riefenstahl make her famous film *Olympische Spiele*?

13. How many times does a runner have to jump the water in an Olympic steeplechase?

(14) How many gold medals did this athlete win at the 1984 Los Angeles Olympics?

▽

(15) Which American athlete set an astonishing world long jump record at the 1968 Mexico Olympics?

(16) These feet belong to a British athlete. Which one?

▽

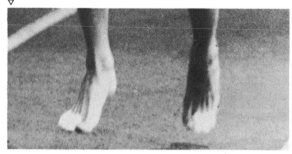

(17) What was the nationality of the winner of the first marathon of the modern Olympics?

(18) How many miles an hour do you have to average to run a four minute mile?

(19) What does the bell rung during the 1500 metre race mean?

(20) How many feet high is the hurdle in front of a runner's steeplechase water jump?

(21) On 26 October 1980 Ernest C. Connor Jnr ran the New York Marathon in a time of 5 hr 18 min. What was so special about his achievement?

(22) How old was America's Bob Mathias when he won the 1948 Olympic decathlon?

(23) What did Coroibus win in the Olympic Games held in July 776 B.C.?

△

(24) On the life of which religious Scottish athlete was this film based?

(25) What nationality is the track star Alberto Juantorena, gold medal winner in both the men's 400 metre and 800 metre track events at the 1976 Olympic Games?

(1) Which is the world's second largest island (if Australia is considered as a continent)?

(2) Which is the most heavily-populated country in Africa?

(3) Which is the smallest of the Great Lakes?

(4) Which is the world's widest river?

(5) Which is the largest bay in the world?

(6) Which country has the most frontiers?

(7) Which desert has the highest sand dunes ever measured?

(8) This is the most photographed, painted and climbed mountain in the world. What is it called?
▽

(9) Which international border is crossed the most?

(10) Which is the world's northernmost national capital?

(11) Which hemisphere has the most countries – the Northern or Southern?

(12) What country is saddled with the ten coldest cities?

(13) What is the name of the world's largest gulf?

(14) This is the world's deepest land gorge. What is it called?
▽

(22) Which is the longest *continuous* frontier in the world?

(23) Which is the world's oldest known walled town?

(24) Which country issued the world's first postage stamp in 1840?

(25) Which of the world's seas is the second largest in area?

(15) These men are guarding the world's smallest independent state. What is it called?

(16) Which is the second largest country on earth, measured by area?

(17) Where in the top ten of the world's highest mountains does the one named after Lt-Col Godwin-Austen come? ▷

(18) Which city has been continuously inhabited for longest?

(19) Which is the third largest lake in the world?
a) Lake Windermere   b) Lake Huron   c) Victoria Nyanza (Lake Victoria)

(20) Which is the world's largest ocean?

(21) Which territory in Asia is the most densely populated in the world?

(1) Which of these actresses said of herself in later life, 'They used to shoot Shirley Temple through gauze. They should shoot me through linoleum'?

a

b

c

(2) In which movie did Lauren Bacall say to Humphrey Bogart, 'If you want anything, just whistle ...'?

(3) Who said that having to make love to Marilyn Monroe was 'like kissing Hitler'?

(4) Which of Charlie Chaplin's films has the opening title, 'A picture with a smile and perhaps a tear'?

(5) With which film is the line, 'Café Mozart, eight o'clock' associated?

(6) Which movie monster uttered the lines, 'Listen to them: children of the night. What music they make ...'?

(7) Who was Joe Pasternak describing when he said, 'Wet she was a star'?

(8) Which great entertainer was known by the catchphrase, 'Goodnight, Mrs Calabash, wherever you are'?

(9) Which of Hollywood's movie moguls was described by B. P. Schulberg as the 'Czar of all the rushes'?

(10) Who was always saying to his colleague, 'Here's another fine mess you've gotten me into'?

(11) Which of Hollywood's leading ladies commented, 'Any girl can be glamorous: all you have to do is stand still and look stupid'?

(12) Who rallies on his deathbed to answer the comment, 'Pity he had no children', with the line, 'Oh, but I have. Thousands of them. And all boys'?

(13) 'There, but for the grace of God, goes God', once snapped Herman Mankiewicz. Of whom was he speaking?

(14) Who was Katharine Hepburn describing when she said, 'He gives her class and she gives him sex'?

(15) What was the famous one-liner that one film critic penned to dismiss *I Am a Camera*?

(16) Which of these dancing stars did Graham Greene sum up as, 'The nearest we are ever likely to get to a human Mickey Mouse'?
a) James Cagney b) Danny Kaye c) Fred Astaire

(17) Which film does Humphrey Bogart appear in when he speaks the line, 'Don't be so sure I'm as crooked as I'm supposed to be'?

(18) Who disliked the image that had brought her success in the 1960s and commented, 'I don't want to be thought of as wholesome'?

(19) Which great Hollywood director is credited with the observation,'Actors are cattle'?

(20) In which of the Marx brothers' films does Groucho say, 'Either this guy's dead or my watch has stopped'?

(21) Which great film of the sea opens with the words, 'Call me Ishmael'?

(22) In which film did Marilyn Monroe do 59 takes of a scene in which her only line was, 'Where's the bourbon?'?

(23) Who made famous the reply in this exchange?
'Goodness, what beautiful diamonds.'
'Goodness had nothing to do with it, dearie.'

(24) Which Hollywood producer wanted 'a story that starts with an earthquake and works its way up to a climax'?

(25) In which of his films does Laurence Olivier say to this woman, 'I'm asking you to marry me, you little fool'?

▷

1 Who took Lee Marvin to court in the celebrated 'palimony' case of 1979?

2 Who went for a swim off Miami and later emerged in Australia with two new names, Joseph Arthur Markham and Donald Muldoon?

3 Who kissed Tom Jones in 1974 and lost the 'world'?

4 Why did Robert Mitchum spend 60 days in jail in 1949?

5 Which two American brothers found the cloud inside their 'silver' lining when the storm broke over their 'bunker' in March 1980?

6 Who offered a fake autobiography of this man to publishers McGraw-Hill in 1971?
▽

7 In which Alpine resort did the French conman and swindler Serge Stavisky end his life in 1934?

8 Who died when Ted Kennedy drove his car off a bridge on Chappaquidick Island on 18 July 1969?

9 She nearly brought down the British government with the Profumo scandal of 1963. Who is she?
▽

10 Who gave French president Giscard d'Estaing the diamonds that led in part to his 1981 electoral defeat?

11 Which member of a European royal family was investigated in 1976 after allegations that he had received bribes from Lockheed?

12 Who was the Duchess of Windsor's first husband?

13 Who was the woman accused of kidnapping Mormon missionary Kirk Anderson in 1977?

14 Which lord went missing after his luck ran out in November 1974?

15 Who was the tennis star arrested with a 14-year-old boy named Bobbie in Beverley Hills in 1946?

16 Who was the Frenchman at the centre of the scandal that provoked Emile Zola to assail the government in his famous article *J'accuse*?

17 Which press tycoon did Marion Davies keep company with for over 30 years?

18 This Hollywood star's image was dented when her daughter wrote *Mommie Dearest* in 1978. What was the daughter's name?

▽

21 Against which European government did Alves Reis perpetrate a massive fraud with forged banknotes in 1925?

22 Which American scandal did this pair uncover in 1972?

▽

19 Which English king illicitly married Mrs Fitzherbert?

20 Whose girlfriend, Nancy Spungen, was found dead in their flat in New York's *Chelsea Hotel* in October 1978, four months before he died of a heroin overdose?

23 Which card game lay at the centre of the Tranby Croft scandal in which the future Edward VII was caught up in 1890?

24 In which country did the financial scandal called the South Sea Bubble burst?

25 The possible murder of which leader forms the theme of David Yallop's book *In God's Name*?

1. Who is this English political leader, who asked to be painted, 'warts and everything'?

▽

2. What words precede, 'And never the twain shall meet'?

3. Who wrote, 'If you can keep your head when all about you are losing theirs ...'?

4. Which psalm begins, 'The Lord is my shepherd'?

5. What did the Wicked Witch of the West write in the sky over the Emerald City?

6. Which book opens, 'At a certain village in La Mancha, which I shall not name ...'?

7. What Jack Kerouac book was described by Truman Capote with the line, 'It isn't writing, it's typing'?

8. The man who drew this cartoon also said, 'A woman's place is in the wrong.' Who is he?

▽

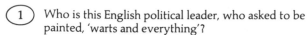

9. Who said, 'Anyone who sees and paints a sky green and pastures blue ought to be sterilized'?

10. Which novel did Bertrand Russell say was, 'all too likely to come true'?

11. What is wrong with this quotation from Jane Austen's novel *Pride and Prejudice*: 'It is a truth universally acknowledged, that a single man in possession of a good fortune, must be in want of a diversion.'

12. Which detective thought something was 'quite a three-pipe problem'?

13. In which of his works did J.M. Barrie write, 'To die will be an awfully big adventure'?

14. Which of Charles Dickens's novels opens, 'It was the best of times, it was the worst of times, it was the age of wisdom, it was the age of foolishness ...?'

15 Who is this American woman writer, who told the Chairman of the House Committee on un-American activities, 'I cannot and will not cut my conscience to fit this year's fashions'? ▽

16 Which of her prime ministers confided to Queen Victoria, 'We authors, Ma'am'?

17 Which T.S. Eliot character measured out his life in coffee spoons?
a) Max House   b) Alfred J. Prufrock   c) Mr N.E.S. Café

18 What was Mark Twain referring to when he defined it as, 'Something that everybody wants to have read and nobody wants to read'?

19 Who once reviewed a book with the words, 'This is not a novel to be tossed aside lightly. It should be thrown with great force'?

20 Who opens one of his novels, 'Riverrun, past Eve and Adam's, from swerve of shore to bend of bay, brings us by a commodius vicus of recirculation back to Howth Castle and Environs'?

21 What is the missing age in this quotation, 'When Mr Bilbo Baggins of Bag End announced that he would shortly be celebrating his . . . birthday . . .'?

22 For which controversial book is the scene set with, 'They sprawled along the counter and on the chairs. Another night. Another drag of a night in the Greeks, a beatup all night diner near the Brooklyn Army base'?

23 On which quotation from Pascal did this woman base her memoirs? ▽

24 From which American book does this sentence come; 'I can see by my watch, without taking my hand from the left grip of the cycle, that it is eight-thirty in the morning'?

25 Which of this writer's characters utters the memorable words 'Curiouser and curiouser!'? ▽

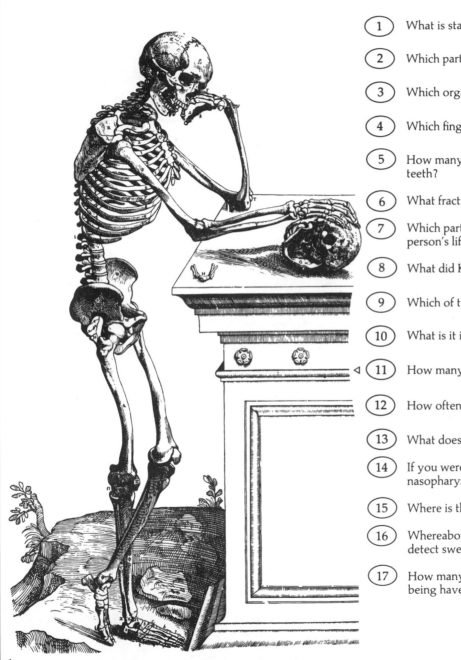

1. What is statistically the safest age of life?

2. Which part of the body is inflamed by hepatitis?

3. Which organ gave us the word 'hysterical'?

4. Which finger boasts the fastest growing nail?

5. How many wisdom teeth are there in a normal set of teeth?

6. What fraction of a person's life passes in sleep?

7. Which part of the eye continues to grow during a person's life?

8. What did Karl Landsteiner divide into four groups?

9. Which of the five senses develops first?

10. What is it impossible to keep open while sneezing?

11. How many bones are there in the human body?

12. How often are brain cells replaced?

13. What does IQ stand for?

14. If you were diagnosed as suffering from acute nasopharyngitis, what illness would you have?

15. Where is the human skin least sensitive?

16. Whereabouts on your tongue are the tastebuds that best detect sweetness?

17. How many pairs of chromosomes does a normal human being have?

(18) What was this giant's name?   ▷

(19) What is a dactyolgram?

(20) What is the common term for the tympanic membrane?

(21) Which vitamin is also called ascorbic acid?

(22) How many times more than the brain does the human body typically weigh?

(23) What is the hardest substance in the human body?

(24) Why is the funny bone so called?

(25) How many sets of children like those shown in the picture did the world's most prolific mother bear?

    ▷

1. In which sport did Russia's Vassily Alexeyev set 80 world records?

2. Who holds the NFL record for most touchdowns in a season?

3. Who succeeded Uwe Seeler as captain of West Germany's national soccer team?

4. What were first used by John L. Sullivan and James J Corbett in 1892?

5. This is a picture of the first playing cricketer to be knighted. Who is he? ▽

6. Who met Ingemar Johansson in world heavyweight title bouts in June 1959, June 1960 and March 1961?

7. Who was elected European Footballer of the Year in 1971, 1973 and 1974?

8. What was the title of this man's autobiography? ▽

9. Who went down for the famous 'long count' in Chicago in 1927?

10. Who was the Chinese-American practitioner of this sport who became a leading star of 'chop socky' movies before dying in 1973 aged 33? ▽

11) Who was the only man to have won the World Drivers' Championship on five occasions?

12) Who pitched a perfect game for the New York Yankees in the 1956 World Series?

13) Of which European country was the British sportsman C.B. Fry allegedly offered the throne?

14) Who was the first golfer to win $100 000 in one year?

15) For which English county cricket side did the great W.G. Grace play?
▽

16) Who was the first player to be elected to Baseball's Hall of Fame?

17) From what material was Dennis Lillie's controversial cricket bat made when he was asked to substitute it in the 1980 Perth test match?

18) What were Babe Ruth's Christian names?

19) How many of his 49 professional fights did Rocky Marciano win?

20) Which Australian was the first tennis player to win two Grand Slams?

21) Which British football star had a father called the 'Fighting Barber of Hanley'?

22) Who holds the record for the greatest number of medals won in Olympic swimming competitions?

23) Whose real name is Edson Arantes do Nascimento?

24) Which Scottish racing driver noted, 'In my sport the quick are often listed among the dead'?

25) At which boxing weight did this famous fighter become world champion in 1980?
▽

(1) France still has one overseas territory in South America. What is its name?

(2) On which group of islands off the coast of South America would you expect to see these creatures?

▷

(3) Which British sea captain explored Burrard inlet on North America's west coast? There is now a city named after him close by.

(4) Where in Peru can you see these lines?

▽

(5) Which is the smallest country in Central America?

(6) How many Canadian provinces border the Great Lakes?

(7) After Canada and Mexico which country is closest to the USA?

(8) Which country is named after the line of latitude that runs through it?

(9) Which South American city was designed by Lucio Costa in the shape of an aeroplane?

(10) What is the principal mineral export from Bolivia?

(11) Which South American country's name means 'Little Venice' in English?

(12) What is the name of the archipelago at the southern tip of South America?

(13) Which river flows through the Grand Canyon?

(14) Which American state borders only one other?

(15) From which country did this craft set out on its famous voyage in 1947?

▷

16   In what year did the Pilgrims first land in America?

17   Which is the oldest capital city in the Americas?

18   Which river is known as the 'Father of Waters'?

19   Which South American country took its name from the Latin for silvery?

20   Which American state capital has more than 30 Buddhist temples?

21   Which New England state doesn't border the Atlantic?

22   Which two South American countries don't border Brazil?

23   Which is the only one of the Great Lakes without an international border running through it?

24   What is the name of the highest waterfall in South America?

25   In which New York building is this famous auditorium to be found?

▽

1. Which 1968 Zeffirelli film starred Leonard Whiting and Olivia Hussey in the title roles?

2. Who played the part of Captain America in *Easy Rider*?

3. Which actress was caught in David Hemmings's photograph in *Blow Up*?

4. In what film did Marlon Brando butter-up Maria Schneider?

5. Which Alfred Hitchcock film was based on a 1959 book by Robert Bloch?

6. How many Oscars were awarded for *A Hard Day's Night*?

7. Which Greek actress played the part of the prostitute who had one day off a week, in *Never On A Sunday*?

8. Who composed the music for Charlie Chaplin's films from 1931 onwards?

▽

△

9. To which twenties sex symbol does this cleavage belong?

10. Donald Sutherland obviously knew in advance that this film was going to be a flop. What was it called?

▽

△

11) For which movie did Cher win the award for Best Actress at the 1985 Cannes film festival?

12) Which American disc jockey played himself in *American Graffiti*?

13) What nationality was the first actress to appear on screen in the nude?

14) Which country heads the world for the greatest number of feature films produced in a year?

15) In which 1944 Jean-Louis Barrault film did he play the great mime artist Deburau?

16) Which German director scored a success with the movie *The Marriage of Maria Braun*?

17) Who portrayed Sarah, Paul Newman's fiancée, in Alfred Hitchcock's *Torn Curtain*?

18) Whose silent film about Napoleon enjoyed a remarkable revival in the 1980s?

19) Which 1962 war film recreated the Normandy landings of June 1944?

20) Which film 'booted' *Singing In The Rain* back into cinemas in 1971?

21) Which film had Mia Farrow and John Cassavetes facing the prospect of bringing up a little devil?

△

22) Who is this well-known Italian actress?

23) Which member of the Marx Brothers once tried to adopt Shirley Temple?

24) Which Russian director made the movie *The Battleship Potemkin*?

25) In which of the James Bond movies did this actor chauffeur 007?

▽

1. Who made the first non-stop transatlantic crossing by aeroplane?

2. Who was the first European to command a ship that sailed into what is now New York Harbour?

3. What significant first has Sidney Poitier achieved here?

4. Who was *Playboy*'s first centrefold model?

5. Who was the first American president born in the 20th century?

6. Which island was Napoleon's first home in exile?

7. Who was made the first honorary citizen of the USA?

8. What was the code-name of the first atom bomb dropped on Hiroshima?

9. Who was the first member of Britain's royal family to graduate from university?

10. What body of water was John Fairfax the first to row across solo?

11. What was the first book set in type?

12. According to the popular song, what did my true love give to me on the first day of Christmas?

13. What is the first Commandment?

14. What notable first is associated with this movie?

15. What means of protecting buildings from storm damage was Benjamin Franklin the first to devise in the early 1750s?

16. Who was the first British monarch to visit New Zealand?

17. Whose 'faith' was rewarded in his 1963 hit *The First Time*?

18. Who was the first incumbent American president to survive being shot?

(19) What is the name of the first sound cartoon featuring this character? ▷

(20) What is about to happen for the first time in this picture?
▽

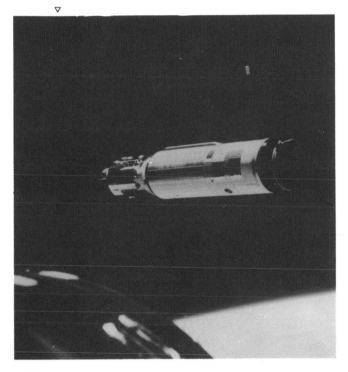

(21) What was the first X-rated film to win an Academy Award for Best Picture?

(22) Who married this woman for the first time in 1964? ▷

(23) Which was the first American state to ratify the Constitution?

(24) Which movie did Cecil B. de Mille direct first in 1923 and again in 1956?

(25) Which was the first western, made in 1962, to be shot in three lens Cinerama?

(1) Where was the boy standing in the poem by Mrs Hemans?

(2) Which shy American poetess wrote more than a thousand poems in secret?

(3) Who wrote *The Ballad of Reading Gaol*?

(4) In which great building in London is Poet's Corner?

(5) What British poet has his own national day?

(6) What American poet showed a preference for lower case typography in works such as *a sweet spontaneous earth*?

(7) Who was appointed England's first official poet laureate by Charles II?

(8) What was the name of the 'sacred river' that flowed through Coleridge's Xanadu?

(9) Who wrote in her poem *Sacred Emily*, 'Rose is a rose is a rose is a rose'?

(10) Which English poet became insane in 1837, when he was barely 40, and died in an asylum in 1864?

(11) What was Robert Browning's wife's maiden name?

(12) From which American poem do these lines come:
'Laugh and the world laughs with you
Weep and you weep alone'?

(13) What did Minnehaha's name mean in English?

(14) Which American poet told an audience in 1935, 'Writing free verse is like playing tennis with the net down'?

(15) Who wrote the poem *An die Freude*, which Beethoven later set to music in his choral symphony?

(16) This poet's face was once described as being '... like a wedding cake left out in the rain'. Who is he?
▽

17 On which Greek island is this poet buried?

▽

18 Who wrote an ode to one of these?

19 What did Andrew Marvell warn his mistress he heard 'hurrying near'?

20 What was T.S. Eliot's middle name?

21 Who, according to Stevie Smith, '. . . has no bosom and no behind'?

22 Who was the poet who popularized the limerick?

23 Which English Romantic poet was drowned off the coast of Italy when his small boat sank in 1822?

24 With whom did Wordsworth join forces to write *Lyrical Ballads*?

25 Which English poet painted this?

▽

(1) Which chemical takes its name from this 'explosive' Swedish chemist?

▽

▷

(7) This man's most famous formula is $E = mc^2$. Who is he?

(8) What turns blue litmus paper red?

(9) What important contribution to science did Dimitri Mendeleyev publish in 1869?

(2) Why shouldn't you drink H_2SO_4?

(3) A chemist might call this NaCl, but what would a cook know it as?

(4) What is the well-known abbreviation for trinitrotoluene?

(5) Who is this famous scientist, making investigations into ▷ light?

(6) Which molecule did James Watson and Francis Crick unravel in 1944?

20. What is the primary colour with the shortest name?

21. Joseph Priestley discovered the gas in 1774, and this French composer wrote the music named after it just over two centuries later. What is the gas?

22. What is the simplest gem in chemical composition?

23. In which movie does this scientist invent a time machine?

10. Which is the world's largest chemical company?

11. If you add Epsom salts to water, does it make the water harder or softer?

12. What term applies to space devoid of matter?

13. What did medieval alchemists seek to achieve?

14. What is quicksilver?

15. Over three-quarters of the air we breathe is made up of one gas. Which is it?

16. What is known as the universal solvent?

17. What is the alloy of copper, zinc and nickel in proportions 6:3:1 known as?

18. What is the boiling point of water at sea level on the Centigrade scale?

19. To what use was nitrous oxide first put by Horace Wells in 1844?

24. Earth, air and water were three of the ancient scientists' 'elements', but what was the fourth?

25. What name is given to the alloy produced from smelting copper with tin?

1. Who did Boris Becker beat to win the men's singles at Wimbledon in 1985?

2. Which European royal family has been closely associated with the tennis competition frequently called the King's Cup?

3. How old was Bobby Riggs when Billy Jean King beat him in their famous male *v.* female match in September 1973?
a) 55 b) 58 c) 63

4. What is the women's equivalent of the Davis Cup competition?

5. Which Parisian art gallery is located in a former tennis court?
▽

6. Which woman player won 22 titles (including 11 singles) between 1960 and 1973 in the tennis championships held in her own country?

7. Who holds the record for winning seven American men's singles titles in a row?

8. Which American tennis player became the youngest player in an event at the French Championships?

9. What is Pancho Gonzales's first name?

10. How long is a tennis court from base line to base line?

11. Which Romanian tennis player became Mrs Bjorn Borg?

12. Which internationally successful tennis twins were born in La Crosse, Wisconsin on 8 September 1951?

13. What do the initials WCT stand for in tennis circles?

14. What tennis first did Don Budge achieve in 1938?

15. Who is this player, the first to achieve the women's singles Grand Slam in 1953?
▽

(16) In which film does this game of tennis take place?
▽

(17) After which year did tennis disappear from the programme of Olympic competitive events?

(18) In which year was a WCT doubles tournament introduced?

(19) Who became the youngest player to win an American singles title in 1979?

(20) Under how many different nationalities did Jaroslav Drobny compete in the Wimbledon championships?
a) 2   b) 3   c) 4

(21) Who came from the Cameroon to become France's top tennis player in 1982?

(22) Who were the brother and sister who won the Wimbledon mixed doubles title in 1980?

(23) Which is the oldest national tennis association in the world?

△

(24) Which country do these players come from?

(25) Jimmy Connors won the Wimbledon men's singles for the first time in 1974. When did his second title come in that event?

(1) Which part of China is nicknamed 'The Roof of the World'?

(2) Which Asian country has the official name Bharat?

(3) What road built during World War II linked Lashio in Burma to Chunking in China?

(4) What is the name of the largest Japanese island?

(5) Which two countries share the Khyber Pass?

(6) Which Asian city is served by Dum Dum airport?

(7) In which notable movie set in India was this actor one of the stars?
▽

(8) Which two Asian countries went to war on 7 July 1937?

(9) In and around which great Chinese city did J.G. Ballard set his novel *Empire of the Sun*?

(10) What was re-named Ho Chi Minh City in 1975?

(11) Of which country is Jakarta the capital?

(12) February is one of the two months in which the Chinese New Year is likely to fall, which is the other?

(13) Which central Asian city became Tamerlane's capital in the 14th century?
▽

(14) On the shore of which sea is the Soviet city of Baku?

(15) Of which country was the king head of state in the musical *The King and I*?

(16) What is the name of the longest river in Asia?

(17) Which country is bordered by Lebanon, Syria, Jordan and Egypt?

(18) Where would you expect to see this sight? ▷

(19) Which of these island groups used to be called the Spice Islands?
a) Moluccas b) Maldives c) Malvinas

(20) What is the principal religion on the island of Bali?

(21) Which oriental religion was founded by Guru Nanak?

(22) What is the unit of currency in Pakistan?

(23) What is the opposite of the Orient?

(24) Along which of China's frontiers did this famous ▷ defensive line run?
a) north b) south c) east d) west

(25) This ancient city was the capital of the Khmer empire. What is it called?
▽

1. How is the sound produced from an aeolian harp?

2. Which musical instrument did Sherlock Holmes play?

3. What does the musical term 'largo' mean?

4. Which instrument was invented by Robert Moog?

5. Who set fire to his guitar for the first time at Finsbury Park on 31 March 1967?

6. Which former bass player for the Silver Beatles died of a brain haemorrhage in 1962?

7. Who taught George Harrison to play the sitar?
▽

8. Which group did Ian Anderson gain fame playing the flute for?

9. Which guitar player was the last act of the Woodstock concert?

10. What colour was The Lemon Piper's tambourine?

11. What tiny musical instrument did this clown habitually take from an enormous case?

12. Which Italian city was home to the Stradivarius family?

13. Who invented the saxophone?

14. For which instrument was Vaughan Williams the first to compose a concerto, in 1954?

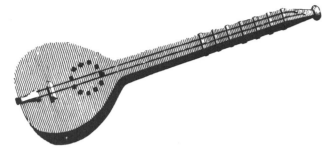

15 What kind of instrument is this?

16 What kind of 'musical' scholarship did this star win to Oxford University?

21 Which instrument did this British film star play?

22 Which song writer has sold more single records than any other?

23 Which country has the world's oldest national anthem?

24 Which orchestral instrument has been described as 'the ill woodwind that no-one blows good'?

25 Who was known as The Swedish Nightingale?

17 Which famous concert pianist also served as Prime Minister of Poland from 1919 to 1920?

18 Which singer received a fee of $1.5 million for one show in San Bernadino County, California on 26 May 1983?

19 Which city boasts the world's largest opera house?

20 Which of the world's most popular songs was sung in space by the astronauts on board *Apollo IX* on 8 March 1969?

(1) Of which Californian town was this man elected mayor in April 1986?

▽

△

(10) What is the name of this bungling policeman?

(11) Who was the only American president to be impeached?

(12) Was Jack the Ripper believed to have been right or left-handed?

(2) Which European country was paralyzed by student riots in May 1968?

(3) Who exclaimed after being shot, 'Why did they do it?'?

(4) Who was 'the law west of the Pecos'?

(5) Who was the lawman who hunted down Billy the Kid in 1881?

(6) Bob Masterson was one of two famous lawmen in Dodge City. Who was the other?

(7) Who were England's 'Bobbies' named after?

(8) Which king was forced to witness the signing of Magna Carta in 1215?

(9) Which American president was the target of two assassination attempts in 17 days?

(13) What has to be produced in a writ of 'habeas corpus'?

a)

b)

(14) In which of Dickens's novels does one of the characters refer to the law as an ass?

(15) To which country were 75 000 convicts shipped between 1790 and 1840?

(16) What was Ted Kennedy convicted of in the Chappaquidick incident?

(17) Who did Giuseppe Zanagara try to assassinate in Miami on 15 February 1933?

(18) Who played the cop among the Amish in the movie *Witness*?

(19) Which of these TV policemen had a hit record with *If* ? ▷

(20) Whose execution provided the inspiration for Norman Mailer's book *The Executioner's Song*?

(21) Which amendment to the American Constitution enshrines the right to keep and bear arms?

◁ (22) The laws of which nation govern life in this European territory?

(23) Whose law states, 'If anything can go wrong, it will'?

(24) From which ancient civilization does the oldest surviving legal code come?

(25) What invention is the subject of the longest patent ever filed in the UK?

(1) What is the third letter of the Greek alphabet?

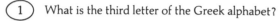

(2) What is the Spanish word for black?

(3) What language boasts the largest vocabulary?

(4) What does the Latin '*quo vadis*' ask?

(5) What is the singular of scampi?

(9) What is the name of this important stone?

(10) What word is used in Hawaii as both a greeting and a farewell?

(6) What is considered the sister language of English?

(7) What letter ends all Japanese words not ending with a vowel?

(8) What is the first letter of the Russian alphabet?

(11) In which direction is Arabic written?

(12) What is the Hungarian word for pepper?

(13) What Hebrew word means 'so be it'?

(14) What was the language of *1984*?

(15) What does *blitzkrieg* mean?

(16) What language is *Stern* magazine published in?

(17) How many letters are there in the Greek alphabet?

(18) What mid-day nap takes its name from the Spanish word for 'sixth'?

(19) Which of the world's alphabets has the greatest number of letters?

(20) What is the word for 'tea' in Chinese?

(23) Whose motto is the German 'Ich dien'?

(24) Where is Manx spoken?

(25) What is the connection between these men and the Japanese word for 'divine wind'?

(21) What does the word 'esperanto' mean in Esperanto?

(22) What is a *billet-doux*?

(1) How many years are there in a millennium?

(2) What are the Roaring Forties?

(3) What is 70 per cent of 70?

(4) How many sides has a dodecagon?
a) 12 b) 20 c) 200

(5) What number can't be represented in Roman numerals?

(6) What ancient measure is the distance from the elbow to the tip of the middle finger?

(7) What line on a map connects all points of the same elevation?

(8) What was Tennyson describing when he wrote:
'Half a league, half a league,
Half a league onward'?

(9) What is the only prime number that is even?

(10) Which vital statistic did these two ladies share?
▽

△

(11) How high was this famous Parisian landmark when it was first erected?
a) 500 ft (152.4 m) b) 985 ft (300.53 m)
c) 1148 ft (349.91 m)

(12) How many land miles are there in a league?

(13) What term does the computer word 'bit' derive from?

(14) Who played the hero in the 1978 film version of John Buchan's The Thirty-Nine Steps?

(15) What is the significance of the title of Ray Bradbury's novel Fahrenheit 451?

(16) What is a gross?

(17) What does the prefix hecto- mean?

(18) What imperial measurement is equal to 0.3048 of a metre?

(19) How many zeros are there in an American trillion?

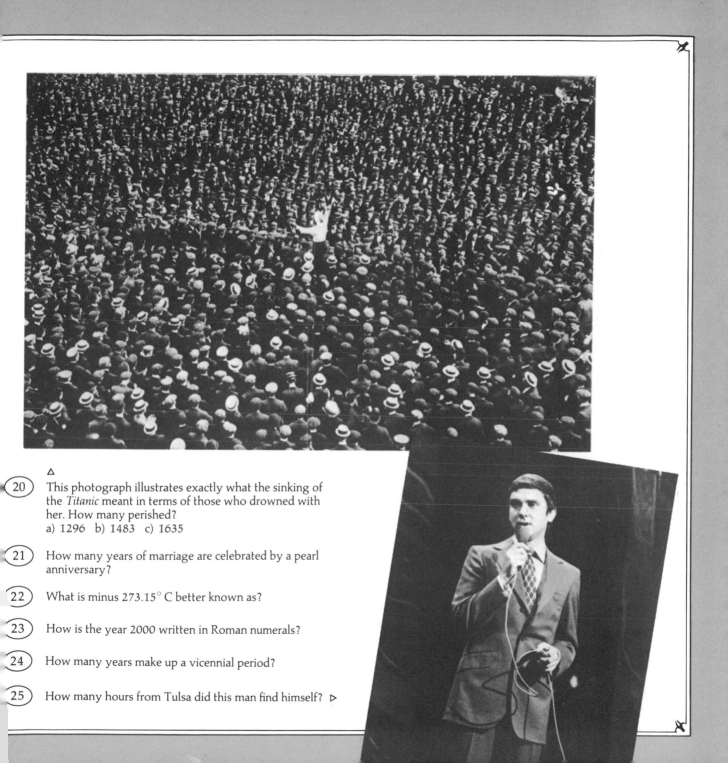

△

(20) This photograph illustrates exactly what the sinking of the *Titanic* meant in terms of those who drowned with her. How many perished?
a) 1296 b) 1483 c) 1635

(21) How many years of marriage are celebrated by a pearl anniversary?

(22) What is minus 273.15° C better known as?

(23) How is the year 2000 written in Roman numerals?

(24) How many years make up a vicennial period?

(25) How many hours from Tulsa did this man find himself? ▷

1. What was the name of the jockey featured in the film *Champions*?

2. What ends when the winner breasts the tape?

3. What did this boxer first change his name to?
▽

4. Who stopped Bjorn Borg's string of Wimbledon singles titles at five?

5. Who was World Snooker Champion from 1927 to 1946?

6. Which jockey won $3 052 146 in 1967?

7. On which of the world's race tracks was this famous ▷ racing driver killed?

8. What was Roger Bannister's number when he broke the four-minute mile barrier?

9. Which motorcycle racing event lost its World Championship status in 1980?
a) 50 cc   b) 350 cc   c) 750 cc

10. Who was the world heavyweight boxing champion for 11 years, 8 months and 12 days?

11. When cheetahs were raced against greyhounds in London in 1937, which animals emerged the winners?

12. What net game sees its women's world amateur champions receive the Uber Cup?

13. What nationality is Ivan Mauger, winner of three consecutive world speedway titles?

14. Which boxer's name translates as 'Praiseworthy the most high'?

15. Which national team has won the World Angling Championships a record number of times?

16 Which sentimental Sunday in 1973 saw Bobby Riggs defeat Margaret Court in straight sets?

17 What colour jersey does the leader wear in the Tour de France? ▷

18 What facial feature was Mark Spitz talking about when he said, 'It acts as a kind of shield. The water slides off it ... and I can go faster'?

19 Who is the tennis player holding the trophy on the right of the picture?
▽

20 Which world famous footballer was born in Lourenço Marques, Mozambique on 25 January 1942?

21 In what sporting event has Franz Klammer won more World Cup races than any other man?

22 The world's longest championship chess match was played between two Russian champions. One was Kasparov, who was the other?

23 Which country produced three British Open Squash champions who together held the title from 1950 until 1963?

24 These Japanese athletes are grappling for the Emperor's Cup. What is their sport?
▽

25 In what sport was Larry Mahan world champion from 1966 to 1970 and again in 1973?

(1) Which Italian landmark has a total of 296 steps?

(2) Which Kenyan city is the safari centre for East Africa?

(3) Which country does the tourist paradise of Bali belong to?

(4) Which city would you visit to look at Wenceslas Square?

(5) Which South American city is overlooked by a statue of Christ 82 ft (25 m) high?

(6) Which city's old quarter is called the Plaka?

(7) Where is the famous Hall of Mirrors?

(8) Which American state is known as 'The Land of 10 000 Lakes'?

(9) Which of the world's museums houses the Elgin Marbles and the Rosetta Stone?

▽

(10) What takes place every July in Pamplona?

(11) In which of the world's great churches is this ceiling to be found? ▷

(12) What is inscribed on the tablet held by the Statue of Liberty?

(13) What is the name of the Soviet Union's state-run travel bureau?

(14) Which Indian city is the home of the Taj Mahal?

(15) Which country would you have to visit today to see the ruins of Troy?

(16) What botanical marvel did Nebuchadnezzar order to be built?

(17) What is the name of this famous Venetian bridge?
▽

(18) Which capital city is home to the statue called the Mannekin-Pis?

(19) What nationality was the founder of this famous travel company?
▽

△

(22) In which English county is this prehistoric monument?

(23) Which is the only one of the Seven Wonders of the Ancient World still standing?

(24) What would you go to Xian in China to see?

(25) In which of the world's capitals can you visit a Disneyland?

(20) Whose husband is this well-known landmark named after?   ▷

(21) In which city is the Wailing Wall?

1. What was unusual about Stravinsky's Circus Polka Ballet?

2. What is Peggy Hookham better known as?

3. Which of his ballets did Tchaikovsky never see as we know it?

4. Which two actresses starred in the ballet film *The Turning Point* in 1977? ▷

5. Who founded London's Royal Ballet School?

6. Who was the classical ballerina star of *An American in Paris*?

7. Where was Nijinsky originally buried?

8. What nationality is dancer Peter Schaufuss? ▽

9. Who is Odette's alter-ego in *Swan Lake*?

10. To which *enfant terrible* of the dance world does this bottom belong? ▽

11. With whom did George Raft star in the movies *Rumba* and *Bolero*?

12. What was the most popular dance at Covent Garden Opera House during World War II?

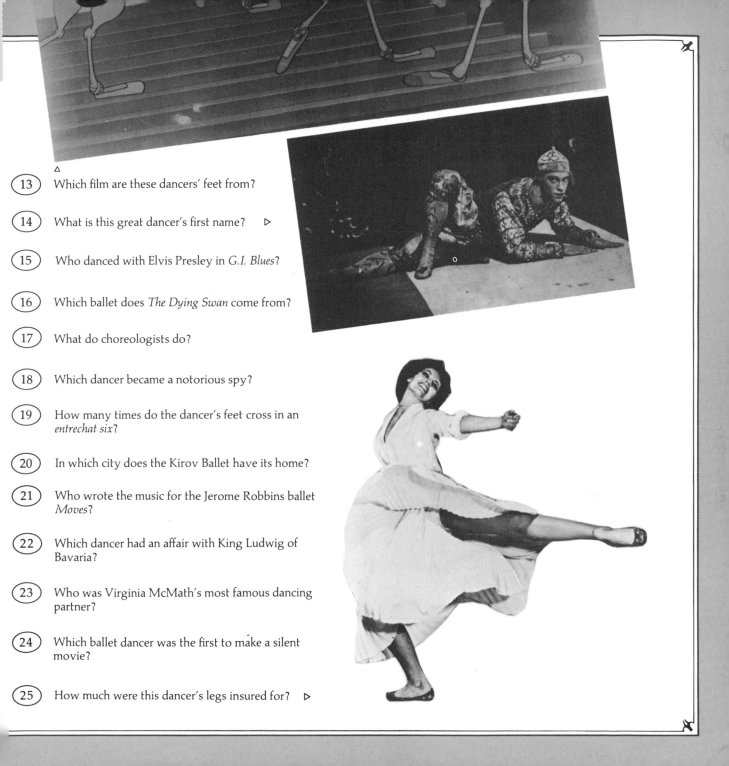

(13) Which film are these dancers' feet from?

(14) What is this great dancer's first name? ▷

(15) Who danced with Elvis Presley in *G.I. Blues*?

(16) Which ballet does *The Dying Swan* come from?

(17) What do choreologists do?

(18) Which dancer became a notorious spy?

(19) How many times do the dancer's feet cross in an *entrechat six*?

(20) In which city does the Kirov Ballet have its home?

(21) Who wrote the music for the Jerome Robbins ballet *Moves*?

(22) Which dancer had an affair with King Ludwig of Bavaria?

(23) Who was Virginia McMath's most famous dancing partner?

(24) Which ballet dancer was the first to make a silent movie?

(25) How much were this dancer's legs insured for? ▷

(1) In which month in 1986 did runners in 76 countries begin the 'Race Against Time'?

(2) In which year did the Pony Express begin operations?
a) 1840 b) 1860 c) 1880

(3) In which year did Adolf Hitler become chancellor of Germany?

(4) When was the Battle of Stamford Bridge fought?

(5) In what month was the atom bomb dropped on Hiroshima?

(6) In which year did the first man walk on the moon?
a) 1967 b) 1969 c) 1971

(7) In which year was this famous lady born?
▽

(8) In which year was Jerusalem finally released from Moslem rule?
a) 1717 b) 1817 c) 1917

(9) What happened in Ireland on 11 July 1690?

(10) When did this well-known writer drown herself?
▷

(11) In which year did this man win the first single-handed transatlantic yacht race?
a) 1958 b) 1959 c) 1960 ▽

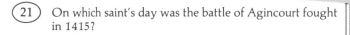

12 Who is this man, who flew into the history books in 1927? ▷

13 Which famous company was founded in 1670?

14 What landmark was created in the history of flying in 1783?

15 In which year did the American space shuttle *Columbia* take off for the first time?

16 In which year was smallpox considered to be eradicated?
a) 1968 b) 1975 c) 1979

17 When were the Nobel prizes first awarded?

18 When was the Panama Canal opened?
a) 1914 b) 1918 c) 1922

19 When did this quartet release *From Me To You*?
a) 1963 b) 1964 c) 1965
▽

20 Which historic book was compiled in 1086?

21 On which saint's day was the battle of Agincourt fought in 1415?

22 What happened in India on the last day of October 1984?

23 In which year were the first Winter Olympic Games held?

24 In which month of 1967 did Israel fight its Six Day War?

25 In which year did Concorde makes its first scheduled supersonic flight?
a) 1972 b) 1976 c) 1979

1   Which English artist had the forenames Joseph Mallord William?

2   Which method of painting takes its name from the Italian for 'fresh'?

3   Which great painter was born and died on the same day in 1483 and 1520 respectively?

4   How many self-portraits did this artist paint?
▽

5   How long did it take Michelangelo to paint the ceiling of the Sistine Chapel?

6   On which Mediterranean island was El Greco born?

7   Which 18th-century English portrait painter once painted a man with two hats?

8   What was Rubens's first name?

9   Which Renaissance painter proved his merit by drawing a perfect circle?

10   How many people appear in Leonardo da Vinci's *The Last Supper*?
▽

11   Which Italian artist painted this Venus?
▷

12 Which country claims Rubens, Van Dyck and Brueghel as citizens?

13 What facial feature doesn't feature on the *Mona Lisa*?

14 Which Italian artist is noted for his paintings of London?

15 Which great master did Charles Laughton portray in one of his films made in 1936?

16 Where is Michelangelo's *Pieta*?

17 Which Spanish painter, when he was only 24, achieved the royal patronage of Philip IV?

18 Which French painter did Napoleon appoint as his court painter in 1804?

19 Who painted this picture?
▽

20 What was the Christian name shared by the 16th-century Dutch painters, the Brueghels?

21 Which Dutch artist was the subject and inspiration for the remarkable forgeries of Hans van Meegeren?

22 Who wrote *Lives of the Painters*?

23 Which Italian Renaissance painter is the subject of a film by Derek Jarman?

24 Which English monarch was Hans Holbein the Younger's royal patron?

25 Who was the English artist who drew this?
▽

(1) What do gorillas do when they get nervous?

(2) Which venomous serpent is known as 'The gentleman among snakes'?

(3) Which is the largest feline?

(4) Which King of Scotland was inspired by a relative of this creature?
▽

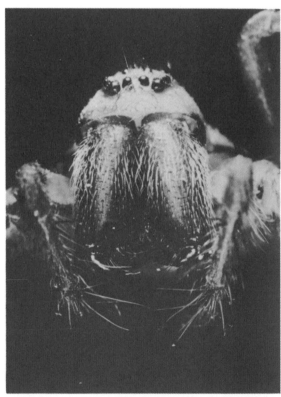

(5) Which is the longest living land mammal after man?

(6) Which animal lives in a lodge?

△

(7) What sort of big cats are these?

(8) How many of the so-called great apes have tails?

(9) What does a stallion have that a gelding used to?

(10) What is the only native North American marsupial?

(11) Which animal has the longest life span in captivity?

(12) To which family does this Andean animal belong?
▽

(13) How many knees does an elephant have?

(14) Which mammal has a bill, webbed feet with claws, and lays eggs?

(15) What is a *canis lupus*?

(16) Which writer explained how the camel got its hump?

(17) What does the name *aardvark* mean in English?

(18) What colour is a white rhinoceros?

△

(24) What name does Beatrix Potter give to this animal in her stories?

(25) Which civilization's gourmets used to consider this creature a delicacy?

▽

(19) To which family of animals does the gnu belong?

(20) What is the only female animal that has antlers?

(21) Which two features are longer on a hare than a rabbit?

(22) What is the more familiar name of the Himalaya's yeti?

(23) Which mammal is considered to have the highest blood pressure?

1. Which casino gambling game means 'railroad' in French?

2. Which jack in a deck of cards is said to represent the Trojan prince Hector?

3. How many playing pieces does each Backgammon player start with?

4. What is the highest hand in Five-Card Draw Poker with wild cards?

5. How many points does it take to win a cribbage game?

6. Who ran this, the 'oldest established moveable crap game in New York'?

▽

△

7. What was this man's favourite card game?

8. Which American city boasts the world's largest casino?

9. Which game is fatal to anyone over 21?

10. What was a California prayer book to an Old West gambler?

11. Which is the higher poker hand, two pairs or three of a kind?

(12) What number do the opposite sides of a dice cube always add up to?

(13) What name did H.S. Mills give to his forerunner of these modern machines?

▽

(16) What are the highest paying odds on a roulette wheel?

(17) Who was the actor stung in *The Sting*?

(18) What denomination coin did most Las Vegas slot machines take in 1981?

(19) What is a Craps player called?

(20) How much is a 'big nickel' to a gambler?

(21) What casino game are you least likely to win at, according to the percentages?

(22) What are the only three Blackjack totals you can double up on in a London casino?

(14) Who was shot down with a pair of aces and a pair of eights in his Poker hand while playing in Deadwood, South Dakota in 1876?

(15) What is the more common name used today for Housey-Housey?

(23) How high do the numbers go in standard Bingo?

(24) Which casino game has the house percentage fixed at 1.27 per cent?

(25) How many dice are used in Poker Dice?

(1) What is the largest lake in Africa called?

(2) By what name is the former Belgian Congo now known?

(3) Which ocean does Mauretania border?

(4) Which national capital is sited where the Blue Nile and the White Nile converge?

(5) What country was known as the Spice Island?

(6) In which African country is the city of Casablanca?

(7) What was the Egyptian city named in the title of Lawrence Durrell's 'Quartet'?

(8) Which West African country takes its name from this animal?
▽

(9) Who discovered the Victoria Falls?

(10) Which African kingdom is ruled by Hassan II?

(11) Which country did Morocco, Tunisia and Algeria fight to win their independence?

(12) On whose novel was this 1951 movie, *The African Queen*, starring Humphrey Bogart and Katharine Hepburn, based?
▽

(13) Who was the author of the famous novel, *Cry the Beloved Country*, published in 1948?

(14) What, in addition to its stars, was 'Morocco bound' in the song from the 1942 movie?

(15) What is Africa's largest country, measured by area?

(16) Where in the order of continents, judged by size, does Africa come?

(17) What major island lies 250 miles (400 km) off the south-eastern coast of Africa?

(18) In which African country was the world's highest recorded shade temperature measured?

(19) With which African nation was Billy Carter implicated in 1980?

(20) In which present-day country were the Ashanti wars fought?

(21) Who was the author of *Tarzan of the Apes*?

(22) What does the name given to these animals literally mean?

(23) What was the name of the cross-eyed lion in TV's *Daktari*?

(24) Which European explorer led the first expedition down the Zaire River in 1876–77?

(25) What name were these animals first given in English?

1. Who directed *Apocalypse Now*?

2. From which film was this still taken?

3. Which musical turned out to be the top money making film of the 1960s?

4. Who directed *American Graffiti*?

5. Who wrote the original script for *Rocky*?

6. Who was the first woman to produce, direct, write and star in a major Hollywood film?

7. In how many films has this actor portrayed James Bond?

8. Which 1973 horror film was written by the novelist William Peter Blatty?

9. How many actors and actresses played this character during the making of the film in which he starred?

10 What is the name of this wookie, one of the stars of the
Star Wars trilogy?

▽

△

11 Which 1964 film told the story of the defence of Rorke's
Drift?

12 Which of Charlton Heston's title characters was known
in real life as Rodrigo Diaz de Bizar?

13 What, according to a 1984 film, should you never get
wet or feed after midnight?

14 In which popular 1956 film did Cantinflas play
Passepartout?

15 In which film were the largest number of extras used?

16 Which film did James Dean complete a few days before
he died?

17 Which Johnny Mathis hit did the aliens cause to be
played in *Close Encounters of the Third Kind*?

18 Which 1962 British film ran for two minutes longer than
this film, which for many years was the longest running
talkie?

19 Which film brought to the screen a Kipling story about
Peachy Carnehan and Daniel Dravot?

20 Who collaborated with Francis Ford Coppola to write
the screenplay for *The Godfather*?

21 Who was commissioned to write the *Star Wars* theme?

22 What was Mongo's mount in *Blazing Saddles*?

23 Which James Michener bestseller spawned the musical
South Pacific?

24 Which song did a group of young Nazis give a chilling
rendition of in *Cabaret*?

25 What is the name of Clint Eastwood's co-star, pictured
here?

▽

1. Which war is the background to George Orwell's *Homage to Catalonia*?

2. Which country's air force was destroyed on the ground on the morning of 5 June 1967?

3. Which fighting unit has its headquarters in Corsica?

4. Which war saw the most Americans die?

5. Who challenged Truman's conduct of the Korean War and was fired for it?

6. What was the name of the first nuclear-powered aircraft carrier?

7. Which war did the Potsdam Conference follow?

8. Who used these animals in his military campaign in Italy?
▽

9. Which war was fought by the houses of York and Lancaster?

10. What animals were crucial to Lawrence of Arabia's campaigns in the 1914–18 war?

11. Which war was waged in 57 countries?

12. What was the series of campaigns to wrest the Holy Land from the Muslim Turks known as?

13. What is the longest war in American history?

14. Which two European countries entered the American War of Independence against the British?

15. In which country is the Waterloo battlefield?

16. In which year did this vehicle first go into action?
a) 1916 b) 1899 c) 1912
▽

(17) Which war ended the Austro-Hungarian monarchy?

(18) What was the first name of the inventor who took out the patent for this revolver in 1835?

▽

FIG.1.

FIG.2.

FIG.3.

△

(19) What was the name of this robot (pictured on the right) in this 'war' movie of 1977?

(20) What sort of weapon was a ballista?

(21) Which number between 10 and 20 held particular significance for the end of the First World War?

(22) Which was the longest war in history?

(23) Which of Hollywood's leading men in the 1950s was also the USA's most decorated soldier in history?

◁ (24) With which war was this woman most closely associated?

(25) What line divided the North and the South in the American Civil War?

△

(1) Who were mythology's snake-haired sisters with the petrifying look?

(2) Which animal in Aesop's fable assumed the grapes he couldn't reach were sour anyway?

(3) Into which city was this taken?

▽

(4) How many deeds did Hercules perform to free himself from bondage?

(5) What beautiful youth pined for love of his reflection?

(6) What was the bull's-eye on Achilles?

(7) What was the food of the Greek gods called?

(8) Whose box did Epimetheus open?

(9) Who was the author of the epic *Aeneid*?

(10) Which civilization invented the arch?

(11) Which philosophic schools did Lao-tzu found?

(12) Which 18th-century English poet earned £5000 from his highly successful translation of the *Iliad*?

(13) In which city can one see this monument describing Trajan's military campaigns?

14 Who incited her brother Orestes to avenge her father's murder?

15 Which Roman poet wrote the popular *Metamorphoses*?

16 How did Apollo punish the prophetess Cassandra?

17 Who is regarded as the father of Greek tragedy?

△

18 Which Greek God is this?

△

19 On which Mediterranean island was this activity popular?

20 Which ancient city has the famous Lion Gate?

21 Which was the oldest and simplest of the Greek orders of architecture?
a) Ionic   b) Doric   c) Corinthian

22 Which Lew Wallace novel set in the ancient world was filmed by MGM in 1926 and 1959?

23 Who was the author of *I Claudius* and *Claudius the God*?

24 The events after whose death form the setting for Mary Renault's historical novel *Funeral Games*?

25 What was the name of this Roman gladiator, played here by Kirk Douglas?
▽

(1) What did 80 000 men cut to build Solomon's Temple?

(2) What do trees get ninety per cent of their nutrients from?

(3) What inside corn makes it pop?

(4) Where in a tree does photosynthesis occur?

(5) What is this plant, whose name derives from the French for 'tooth of the lion'? ▷

(6) Which plant is opium derived from?

(7) In which British gardens can you see this building? ▽

(8) Which plant does natural vanilla flavouring come from?

(9) From which part of the cork oak is cork obtained?

(10) What is snuff?

(11) Which Cherokee Indian gave his name to a tree?

(12) What is the connection between this and *Pieris brassicae* ▽

(13) What fungus has a crown, spores, gills and a stalk?

(14) What is missing from a navel orange?

(15) What science did Gregor Mendel establish in 1866?

(16) What name does John Wyndham give to the mobile plants that take over the world in one of his novels?

(23) On which side of a tree are the rings farther apart?
a) north b) south c) east d) west

(24) In which country did the citrus fruit the mandarin originate?

(25) Who was the father of modern botany, who established the system for classifying plants in the middle of the 18th century?

(17) Which trees are commonly found in English churchyards?

(18) In which country are one-quarter of the world's forests located?

(19) Which African country is the home of the world's remotest tree?

(20) Who was author of the novel *Keep the Aspidistra Flying*, published in 1936?

(21) From which flower is saffron obtained?

(22) Which flower is most closely associated with this ▷ entertainer?

1. Where in France is the famous 24-hour motor race held?

2. Which car maker's engines are used in Formula Vee racing?

3. On which British island might you expect to see these races?

▽

4. Which European country is home to the Zandvoort Grand Prix racetrack?

5. Which holiday is the Indianapolis 500 run on?

6. At what site in Utah are land speed records set?

7. Which American won the world Grand Prix driving championship in 1978?

8. Which class of racing has all the cars at 1290 or more pounds (558 k)?

9. What is the term for this kind of racing start?

▽

10. Which motoring movie of 1965 starred Tony Curtis, Jack Lemmon and Natalie Wood?

11. Which country staged the world's first national Grand Prix?

12. In which city was the one and only Yugoslav Grand Prix held in September 1939?

13. In what make of Japanese car did John Surtees win the 1967 Italian Grand Prix?

14. Where in America did a new street race circuit come into being in 1975?

15. Which American hill climb course is the second oldest motor racing speed event in America?

16. Which car did Paddy Hopkirk drive to victory in the 1964 Monte Carlo rally?

17 What was the name of the great Italian motor manufacturer who produced this car?
▽

18 Which motor racing team has the longest unbroken record of participation in Grand Prix racing?

19 Which racing car constructor built the first six-wheel Grand Prix car?

20 Which British racing driver was the first to wear a full safety-harness?

21 With which line of successful racing cars is Colin Chapman's name closely linked?

22 Who is the only driver to win the World Championship driving his own cars?

23 What nationality is the racing driver Jacky Ickx?

24 Who died when the plane he was piloting crashed into a golf course near London in November 1975?

25 What is the official name of this sport?
▽

(1) Who featured the mountain paradise of Shangri-La in his novel *Lost Horizon*?

(2) What were these men the first in the world to do?
▽

(3) Which is the highest mountain in the world outside Central Asia?

(4) By what other name is the mountain called Denali also known?

(5) In which country is Mount Kilimanjaro the highest peak?

(6) On which peak did this vessel come to rest? ▷

(7) Which mountain was traditionally the home of the gods of the ancient Greek pantheon?

(8) Which country has the world's highest capital city?

(9) On which mountain did Moses receive the Ten Commandments?

(10) On which Caribbean island did Mont Pelée erupt in May 1902, killing all but one of the inhabitants of the town of St Pierre?

(11) Which South American city is overlooked by the Sugar Loaf Mountain?

(12) Who was Mount Everest named after?

(13) Which two countries are linked by the Brenner Pass?

(14) Which country would you visit to ski in the Dolomites?

(15) Which mountains separate Europe from Asia?

(16) In which country is the world's tallest self-supporting tower?

(17) In which country does the Salang Road Tunnel pass through a mountain range?

(18) After which American president is New Hampshire's highest mountain named?

19. Which is the only active volcano on the European mainland?

20. Who is the only American president carved on Mount Rushmore wearing glasses?

21. Which of Clint Eastwood's films takes its name from a European peak?

◁ 22. Which building pushed this landmark into third place among the world's tallest inhabited buildings?

23. Who composed and first sang the song *Rocky Mountain High*?

24. Which square does this famous high spot look down on?
▽

25. Which is the world's highest navigable lake?

6 Who is the most successful writer of westerns ever?

◁ 7 Who starred in the title role of the western he made with this leading lady?

8 Which famous western character was played on TV by Jay Silverheels?

9 Who went along with Bronson and Coburn from *The Magnificent Seven* to *The Great Escape*?

10 What was the name of the communication system that linked St Joseph, Missouri with Placerville, California?

11 Who was Hawkeye's Indian friend?

12 Who played Frenchy in the 1939 version of *Destry Rides Again*?

13 What TV series featured the trail boss Gil Favor?

14 Who directed the 1962 western, *The Man Who Shot Liberty Valance*?

15 Who is this wild west pioneer? ▽

1 Which famous gun-lady of the old west has been portrayed on the movie screen by, among others, Jean Arthur in 1936, Jane Russell in 1948 and Doris Day in 1953?

2 Who played the title role in TV's *Bronco*?

3 In which western town did the gunfight at the OK Corral take place?

4 Who was Dale Evans's cowboy husband?

5 Which movie had gunslinger Frank Fuller arriving on the midday train?

△

16 Which Canadian city holds its world famous Stampede every year?

17 Who was the only character, apart from Matt Dillon, to last through *Gunsmoke's* entire run?

18 Who won an Oscar as best actor in the movie *Cat Ballou*?
▽

19 What was the name of Jesse James's outlaw brother?

20 Who played the title role in the long-running series, *The Virginian*?

21 What was Buffalo Bill's real name?

22 Which movie star played *The Electric Horseman* in 1979?

23 Which composer won an Oscar for his song in this western?
▽

24 Who was the box office draw in movies like *Where The North Begins*, *The Clash of Wolves* and *Frozen River*?

25 What was the title of Mel Brooks's 1974 spoof western?

(1) In which national army were these cadets destined to serve?
▽

(2) Which war featured the Charge of the Light Brigade?

(3) At which battle was a horse named Comanche the only survivor on the losing side?

(4) Which British commander surrendered to this man in October 1781?
▷

(5) What was the martial song of the Confederacy in the American Civil War?

(6) Which two commanders directed the opposing forces in the battle of El Alamein?

(7) The Battle of Borodino inspired a famous overture. Which one?

(8) Who led the settlers of Pitcairn Island?

(9) Where did Napoleon suffer his final defeat?

(10) Which country was the scene of the Boxer Rebellion of 1900?

(11) In which African country did this battle take place?
▽

(12) Which European country has been the site of most battles?

(13) In which country did the Mau Mau uprising take place?

(14) At which battle did England's Richard III cry 'my kingdom for a horse', according to Shakespeare?

(15) Who commanded the French forces at the battle of Orléans in 1428?

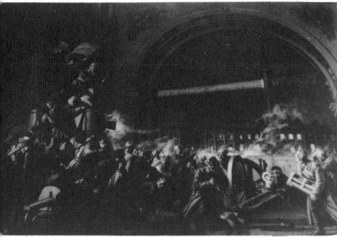

16. What building is being stormed by Bolshevik troops in this picture?

17. On which continent did Allied forces land on 8 November 1942?

18. On which day of the week did the Japanese attack Pearl Harbor?

19. Which middle eastern capital fell to its attackers in 1453?

20. Which sea battle ended Turkish naval power in the Mediterranean in the 16th century?

21. Who commanded the American forces in France during the First World War?

22. Where did this battle occur?

23. With which famous revolution is this man associated?

24. Which World War II offensive is now fought by slimmers?

25. Which emperor instigated the Roman invasion of Britain in AD 43?

(1) Which writer is commemorated by this statue? △

(2) What was John Steinbeck's travelling companion Charley?

(3) What are Henry Miller's two 'tropical' books?

(4) Which George Orwell work contains the line 'Vote for Snowball And The Three Day Week'?

(5) Which former ward attendant in a mental hospital wrote *One Flew Over the Cuckoo's Nest*?

(6) Which Hermann Hesse book gave its name to a rock group?

(7) What was Eric Segal's sequel to *Love Story* called?

(8) Which author named his main character after Oliver Wendell Holmes?

(9) Who is the subject for Irving Stone's *Lust For Life*?

(10) This Russian writer was deported from the Soviet Union in 1974. Who is he? △

(11) Which Joel Chandler Harris book tells the story of Br'er Fox and Br'er Rabbit?

(12) Which book did these twins originate to settle arguments in pubs? ▽

13. Which was the second book of J.R.R. Tolkien's trilogy *The Lord of the Rings*?

14. Which book did Charles Dickens leave unfinished when he died?

15. Which disease caused D.H.Lawrence's early death?

16. Who wrote *Future Shock*?

17. What Henri Charrière best-seller describes his escape from Devil's Island?

18. Whose epitaph reads, 'Quoth the raven nevermore'?

19. Who wrote *Round the Bend*?

20. Who was Thomas Hardy's most 'obscure' character?

21. What James Clavell novel recounts John Blackthorne's adventures in 16th-century Japan?

22. What was the name of an upturned ship in a Paul Gallico adventure?

23. Which Leon Uris novel deals with the Russian capture of Berlin?

24. Which renowned English author had been a Polish sailor?

25. Who got a $50 000 advance to drape 11 000 words around 111 photos of this movie star?

▽

(1) Which insect transmits yellow fever?

(2) What is the most widely used tranquillizer in America?

(3) What is the term for a cancer causing substance?

(4) What are you if you are myopic?

(5) Which disease do the French call 'La Rage'?

(6) Which common ailment can't you catch at the North Pole?

(7) What once-in-a-lifetime moment is happening here?
▽

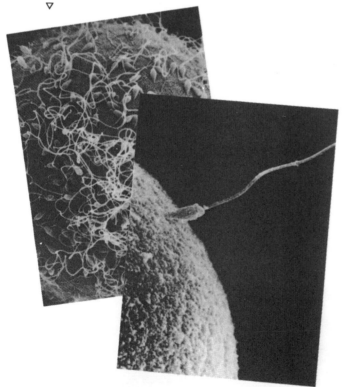

(8) What causes baker's itch?

(9) What was Marcus MD's surname?

(10) What is the common name for acetylsalicylic acid?

(11) What does T.I.D. mean on a doctor's prescription?

(12) What does Salk vaccine prevent?

(13) Which drug was named for Morpheus, the Greek god of dreams?

(14) Why did this doctor have reason to regret the invention of wireless telegraphy?
▽

(15) Which Greek physician is known as 'The Father of Medicine'?

(16) What has caused every human death?

(17) Who played television's Dr Kildare?

(18) What is rubella better known as?

(19) Which disease brought tragedy in this film? ▽

(20) Which sex is twice as likely to contract leprosy?

(21) What caused 20 million deaths in 1918?

(22) Who performed the first successful human heart transplant?

(23) What does ECG stand for?

(24) Which disease did this man die of? ▽

(25) What was the 'Black Death'? ▽

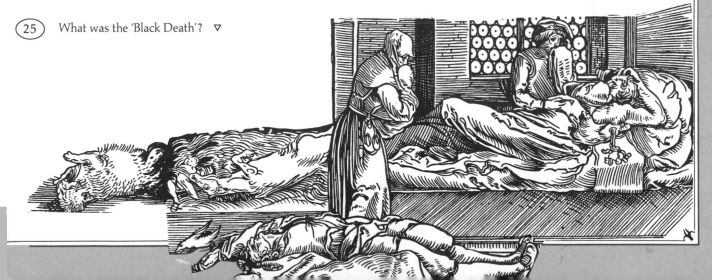

1. Which royal lady was criticized for playing golf in 1567 only two weeks after her husband's death?

2. What is the diameter of a golf hole?

3. Which Australian golfer has been dubbed the Great White Shark?

4. What material were the earliest golf balls made from?

5. Who, in 1965, became the first foreigner in 45 years to win the American Open Golf title?

6. Which European golfer played this shot in the Benson & Hedges tournament at Fulford, York, England in 1981?
▽

7. What is an 'albatross', or 'double-eagle', in golf?

8. In which country is the world's longest golf hole?

9. Which club, on average, hits a golf ball further – a two iron or a three wood?

10. Over which course is the American Masters always played?

11. How many spikes are there on the toe of a standard golf shoe?

12. In which year did this man's classic come to a sticky end?
▽

13. How many golf holes have you played when you're 'at the turn'?

14. Which is the oldest match in the world between two golf clubs?

15. What California resort calls itself 'The Golf Capital of the World'?

16. Before the invention of the tee-peg in 1920, how did golfers tee their balls?

(17) Which golfer wears this cap?
▽

(18) Who is this man, who won the British Open golf title ▷ five of the nine years ending in 1983?

(19) How many inches is the minimum depth of a golf hole?

(20) In which year was a European side first selected to play the American side in the Ryder Cup?

(21) How many minutes does a golfer have to find a lost ball?

(22) Which country has the world's highest golf course?

(23) What is the only major golf tournament Arnold Palmer never won?

(24) What golf stroke is mis-hit when a player suffers from the 'yips'?

(25) In which golf tournament is this trophy awarded to the winner? ▷

(1) Errol Flynn, star of *The Sea Hawk*, is on the right – but what is the name of his primate pal?

▽

(2) The deepest ocean trench on earth lies in the western Pacific, what is its name?

(3) Which *Double-Eagle* made the first balloon crossing of the Pacific in November 1981?

(4) On which body of water does the port of Marseilles lie?

(5) Who commenced a round-the-world voyage as commander of a ship called the *Pelican*?

(6) Which ocean is only one twelfth the size of the Pacific?

(7) Who gave his name to the sea that divides north-east Siberia from Alaska?

(8) In which famous novel of the sea does HMS *Compass Rose* sink?

(9) Into which sea does the River Danube flow?

(10) Which country lies on the northern shore of the Straits of Hormuz?

(11) What is the approximate percentage of the southern hemisphere covered by seas and oceans?
a) 80%   b) 75%   c) 60%

(12) What's the name of this sea-faring villain?

▽

(13) Of which country was Henry the Navigator a prince?

(14) Which ocean surrounds the Sargasso Sea?

15 Which of the world's 'seas' is in fact its largest lake?

16 With what nautical song did this singer have a hit in 1975?
▽

17 On which of these degrees of latitude is it possible to sail all round the world?
a) 40°S   b) 60°S   c) 80°S

18 Which European city was nicknamed the 'bride of the sea'?

19 Who designed this great steamship in conjunction with J. Scott Russell?   ▷

20 What ocean laps at the shores of Madagascar?

21 Who was the ancient Greek god of the sea?

22 What strait divides the Pillars of Hercules?

23 With which other sea does the Bosporus link the Black Sea?

24 Which country has the world's longest coastline?

25 How long are nautical dog watches?

(1) In which American state did this man die?
▽

△

(7) Which band backs this American rock star?

(8) Which famous rock band was originally called Smile?

(9) What are the first names of these brothers?
▽

(2) Which heavy rock band was formed by Robert Plant and Jimmy Page in 1968?

(3) Which group starred in the movie *Rock Around the Clock*?

(4) What was Elvis Presley's middle name?

(5) Which member of The Rolling Stones drowned in a swimming pool on 8 June 1969?

(6) Who is this 'twanging' guitarist?
▷

(10) What was the name of Buddy Holly's backing group?

(11) Which British rocker had his first hit with *Move It*?

(12) What colour did the Rolling Stones want to paint it in 1966?

(13) What links the Monkees' early hits and a band called the Candystore Prophets?

(14) Was this guitarist left or right handed?
▽

△

(15) Who is Vincent Furnier better known as in rock circles?

(16) Which member of Cream was a Yardbird?

(17) Which band kicked off the British part of the Live Aid concert?

(18) Which Elvis Presley movie featured the song *Can't Help Falling in Love*?

(19) Who is the lead singer with The Who?

(20) Which author's works did Mott the Hoople and Steppenwolf take their names from?

(21) Which of this band's albums was named after one of the chapters of *Wind in the Willows*?

(22) Which Louisiana rocker set the world alight with *Great Balls of Fire*?

(23) Which British rocker had a hit album with *The Sound of Fury* in 1960?

(24) Which band consisted of 'Marco, Merrick, Terry Lee, Gary Tibbs and yours truly'?

(25) Babs, Joy – and who was the third member of this sisterly group?
▽

(1) Who was the only English pope?

(2) By what name was Vladymir Ilyich Ulyanov better known?

(3) Of which country was the house of Hapsburg the ruling dynasty?

(4) Who was responsible for nationalizing the Suez Canal?

(5) Which French king was known as the Sun King?

(6) How did Ghazi, King of Iraq, die in April 1939?

(7) What was King David's relationship to King Saul?

(8) This leader was known as the 'Lion of Judah'. Who is he?
▽

(9) What is the origin of the titles Tsar and Kaiser?

(10) Which kingdom had a number of kings called Kamehameha?

(11) Of which country was Jimmu Tenno traditionally the first emperor?

(12) Which king was fond of building castles like these?
▽

(13) Which English king was Unready?

(14) The ruby of which famous prince is now set in the British Imperial State Crown?

(15) Who was the first French-speaking Premier of the Canadian Confederation?

(16) Who was India's first prime minister?

(17) After whom is Malta's capital named?

(18) Who was sent to England by Pope Gregory the Great in AD 597?

(19) Where in the list of American presidents does this man ▷ come?
a) third   b) fifth   c) sixth

(20) This queen reigned for just nine days. What was her name?
▷

(21) Whose clothes has this future head of state borrowed? ▷

(22) Who was nicknamed 'Brandy Nan'?

(23) What nationality was the pope who restored the papacy to Rome from Avignon?

(24) In which European country did the Ayatollah Khomeni spend his last years of exile before returning to Iran?

(25) In which sport did Greece's last king win an Olympic gold medal?

1. What dark realm did the Lord of the Rings call home?

2. Which European country was the first to be A-bombed, by Albania, in Nevil Shute's 1957 novel *On The Beach*?

3. Who wrote the satirical novel set in a crematorium and called *The Loved One* in 1948?

4. What did Joseph Heller rename the adage 'Damned if you do and damned if you don't'?

5. Which futurist novel was originally to have been titled *The Last Man in Europe*?

6. Which novel introduced Instructor Sullivan to Edgar Gull Chiang?

7. What was the 'prime success' of Muriel Spark?

8. Which novel by Mario Puzo did this young actor grow up to star in?

▽

9. What alternative was offered in a Frederick Forsyth novel?

10. Which American university provides the setting for *Love Story*?

11. Which Somerset Maugham novel has been filmed three times?

12. Whose first novel, published in 1949, was called *The Young Lions*?

13. Who was the author of the posthumously published novel *Maurice*?

14. To which town does *A Town Like Alice* refer?

15. What was *But Gentlemen Marry Brunettes* a sequel to?

16. What was the subject of Kyle Onstott's *Mandigo*?

17. In which movie based on a James Leo Herlihy novel did this actor play this character?

▽

18 Who wrote the novel which opens, 'The past is a ▷ foreign country; they do things differently there'?

△

19 To which German air ace was this novelist related by marriage?

20 Who wrote the occult mystery *The Devil Rides Out*?

21 Which Agatha Christie thriller took its title from a line in a poem by Tennyson?

22 What is the surname of the father and son responsible for *Lucky Jim* and *Money* respectively?

23 Which 13¾-year-old published his diaries with great success?

24 Which John Fowles novel was adapted for the big screen by Harold Pinter?

25 This man could be said to be Mrs Thatcher's favourite author. Who is he? ▷

① Who directed the film *2001: A Space Odyssey*?

② Who was the second man to walk on the moon?

③ What was the name of America's first manned space programme?

④ By what name is the SDI popularly known?

⑤ With which number do you associate this cult TV show?
▽

⑥ Which planet did the Mariner spacecraft explore?

⑦ Who was the first man to hit a golf ball on the moon?

⑧ What is believed to be created when a star collapses?

⑨ How many astronauts manned each Gemini flight?

⑩ Which country has the third most satellites in orbit?

⑪ What nationality was the first non-Russian, non-American man to fly in space?

⑫ Which nation launched the Blue Streak rocket?

⑬ What was the first Apollo mission to orbit this planet?
▽

⑭ Which of NASA's lunar modules was the first to land on the moon?

⑮ How many times did John Glenn orbit the earth?

⑯ Who was the first woman to fly in space?

⑰ In which Apollo spacecraft did astronauts Grissom, White and Chaffee perish in January 1967?

(18) From which planet, apart from Earth, did this 'spaceman's' ancestors come?

(19) Who wrote the 1901 novel *The First Men On The Moon*?

(20) Which German scientist perfected and launched the V-2 rocket in World War II?

(21) Who was the first American to walk in space?

(22) How many tiles did the space shuttle *Columbia* lose on its second flight?

(23) Which country did Skylab hit?

(24) Which planet did Viking I land on?

(25) What was the name of this dog, the first to be launched into space?
▽

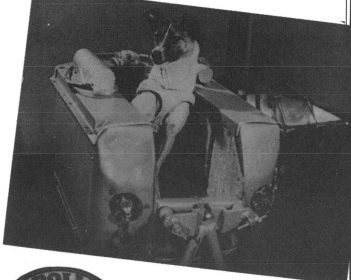

1. Which sherry is sweeter, *fino* or *amoroso*?

2. Which two ingredients make a Black Velvet?

3. What colour is chablis?

4. What do you get when you mix tequila, triple sec and lime juice?

5. What is known as the Queen of Drinks?

6. What does 'trocken' mean on a bottle of German wine?

7. Which spirit was known in 18th-century England as Cuckold's Comfort, Make Shift and Ladies' Delight?

8. What kind of beans are dropped into a *sambucca*?

9. What colour is a Remy Martin bottle?

10. Which vegetable usually provides the lush foliage in a Bloody Mary?

11. Which geometric shape graces the label of a bottle of Bass Pale Ale?

12. Which port has matured longer in wood – Tawny or Ruby?

13. What does 'tafelwein' mean on a bottle of German wine?

14. What is the correct order of consumption of lemon, salt and tequila?

15. What is bottled in jeroboams?

16. What is mixed in a B & B?

17. Which liqueur is a French version of Curaçao?

18. The *Cutty Sark*, pictured here, gives its name to a brand of whisky. Which way is the ship sailing on the label – left or right?

▽

19 Which liqueur is the base for a Copenhagen Mary?

20 What is the most popular cocktail in America?

◁ **21** What is the distinctive shape of these bottles modelled on?

22 In which country was Vinho Verde first produced?

23 Which east European country was the home of the sweet wine called Tokay?

24 What kind of wine did this man invent?

▽

◁ **25** How does this character like his Martini?

(1) Which of the world's national airlines is known by three consecutive letters of the alphabet?

(2) What is the most common colour on the fields of American state flags?

(3) Which international airport is known in the travel world by the code NRT?

(4) How many points are there on the maple leaf on the Canadian flag?

(5) What is the national flower of Austria?

(6) By what symbol was Sir Percy Blakeney known throughout revolutionary France?

(7) Which Asian country has this flag?
▽

(8) Which American state is nicknamed the Bluegrass State?

(9) What are emblazoned on the Jolly Roger?

(10) Which religion was once identified by the sign of the fish?

(11) What in Islam is the equivalent of the cross in Christianity?

(12) What is the name of the mark found on the side of merchant ships?

(13) What single colour constitutes the flag of Libya?

(14) Of which country is this the official animal?
▽

(15) What initials signify a diplomat's car?

△

20. What country's flag has lasted the longest without change?

21. Which bird is the national symbol of France?

22. Which Greek goddess had this bird as her emblem?
▽

23. Which Mediterranean country is the only one to display its map on its flag?

24. What is Florida's nickname?

25. What are the names of the two complementary forces of the universe symbolized in this ancient Chinese sign?
▽

16. What colour is the hammer and sickle on the Soviet Union's flag?

17. Which breed of dog decorates the fleet of inter-city buses that criss-cross the USA?

18. Which vegetable is closely associated with Wales?

19. What do the initials NASA stand for?
▽

1. Which famous cartoon duo first appeared in *Puss 'n' Toots* in 1942?

2. A quartet of what sort of cartoon birds danced with Dick Van Dyke in *Mary Poppins*?

3. Which Disney cartoon film saw two animals eating spaghetti at Tony's restaurant?

4. Which national park did Yogi Bear call home?

5. Which cartoon sheriff of the old west had a look-alike nephew in a Terrytoon series on TV?

6. What does Dumbo swallow that brings on the surrealistic sequence 'Pink Elephants on Parade' in the cartoon film?

7. Which cartoon character asks Elmer Fudd, 'What's up, Doc?', in *A Wild Hare*?

8. In which film does Mickey Mouse appear in this role?
▽

9. What is the name of this cartoon character's baby?
▽

10. Which was the last animated film on which Walt Disney worked?

11. Which Disney cartoon film evolved from Felix Saltern's book about forest life?

12. In which Max Fleischer cartoon did Twinkletoes, the carrier pigeon, and King Bombo make their screen debut?

13. Which was the most expensive Disney cartoon ever made?

14. Which cartoon character made his debut in *Mickey's Revue* in 1932?

15. Which character's first words on the screen were, 'Who — me? Oh no! I got a bellyache!'?

16. Which character in *The Jungle Book* owed his voice to ▷ Phil Harris?

(17) In which cartoon film was this lady the villainess? ▷

(18) Who is 'the fastest mouse in all Mexico'?

(19) What do the initials UPA stand for in the world of cartoons?

(20) Which full-length Disney cartoon earned its creator a special Academy Award in 1938?

(21) Which Hanna and Barbera TV cartoon series, set among New York's alley cats, was an amusing take-off of Sergeant Bilko?

(22) What is the name of the cat forever pursuing Tweety?

(23) Whose voice was Mickey Mouse given in his earliest cartoons?

(24) Who was the woodpecker created by Walter Lantz?

(25) What happens when this character tells lies?
▽

1. Which ancient ruler was the son of Philip of Macedon and his wife Olympias?

2. Who did the Athenians defeat at the Battle of Marathon in 490 BC?

3. Which Roman emperor instigated the invasion of Britain in AD 43?

4. What military man was Hasdrubal's father?

5. Which of the Seven Wonders of the World was built near Alexandria in Egypt?

6. What nationality was this ancient ruler? ▷

7. For what feat of engineering is the Chinese emperor Chin Shih Huang Ti remembered?

8. How many banks of oars were there on a Roman trireme?

9. Which volcano buried the city of Pompeii when it erupted in AD 79?

10. What was the main activity in ancient Rome's Circus Maximus?

11. In its heyday, how many people could this amphitheatre seat?
a) 15 000   b) 30 000   c) 45 000
▽

(12) Which Greek philosopher was the first to describe the lost continent of Atlantis?

(13) Who was the Roman procurator of Judaea and Samaria from AD 26 to 36?

(14) What is the Biblical name for Babylonia?

(15) Julius Caesar and Marcus Crassus were two members of the 'First Triumvirate'. Who was the third?

(16) Which Greek philosopher was 'The Gadfly of Athens'?

(17) Famous examples of what type of ancient construction can still be seen at Segovia in Spain and at the Pont du Gard in southern France?

(18) Who was the first Christian Roman emperor?

(19) Did the Mayan civilization collapse before or after the birth of Christ?

(20) Which great Minoan palace boasts these remains?

(21) Which month of the year is named after the two-faced Roman god of doorways?

(22) What was the Roman name for London?

(23) Which present-day country was Gnaeus Julius Agricola governor of in the first century AD?

(24) Between which Middle Eastern rivers did the ancient civilizations of Mesopotamia flourish?

(25) In which city would you see this building?

(1) Which museum provides a home for the painting generally called *Whistler's Mother*?

(2) In which room did Napoleon keep this painting?

(3) Where are the Pitti and Uffizi art galleries?

(4) Where would you arrive by going second to the right and straight on till morning?

(5) What is the name of the Wilkes plantation in *Gone With The Wind*?

(6) Which fictional character had a mansion at West Egg, Long Island?

(7) How many guns of Navarone were there?

(8) What Anthony Shaffer two-man play opens in the living-room of Andrew Wyke's Norman manor house?

(9) What country is the setting for Edgar Allen Poe's *The Pit and the Pendulum*?

(10) Which river did Dorlcote Mill stand on?

(11) What is the setting for John Le Carré's *A Small Town In Germany*?

(12) Which country provides the setting for the novel *Summer of the Seventh Doll*?

(13) Which English county provided the setting for most of this artist's work?

(14) Which part of Paris featured most prominently in the work of the French impressionists?

(15) Which planet is taken over by aliens called Overlords in Arthur C. Clarke's novel *Childhood's End*?

(16) Where does Ray Bradbury's *Chronicles* take place?

(17) Who carved the famed Medici tombs in Florence?

▽

△

(24) What is the name of this mill?

(25) Where did William Wordsworth compose the lines:
'Earth has not anything to show more fair;
Dull would he be of soul who could pass by
A sight so touching in its majesty.'?

(18) Which of Shakespeare's plays is set in Illyria?

(19) What 1959 Philip Roth novel took place in Columbus, Ohio?

(20) Where is one of George Orwell's works 'down and out'?

(21) What does the painting *The Battle of Gettysburg* claim to be?

(22) Where is the John Paul Getty Museum?

(23) Over which city did the room in this film have a view? ▷

△

7   What does VTOL stand for?

8   Who was the pilot in the first fatal aircrash?

9   Which is the world's largest airline?

10   Which airfield did Charles Lindbergh land at to end his historic transatlantic flight?

11   In which of his films did Richard Todd play Wing Commander Guy Gibson?

12   Which Mediterranean principality staged the first competition for this type of aircraft in 1912?

▽

"You're in a great hurry," bantered Biggles.

1   Where did Phileas Fogg begin and end his trip round the world?

2   Who was the first woman to receive the Distinguished Flying Cross?

3   What must be exceeded to produce a sonic boom?

4   Which city did Jacques Garnerin make his parachute jump over in 1797?

5   How many engines does a Boeing 737 have?

6   Who created this flying ace?   ▷

(13) Which famous flying service was inaugurated at Cloncurry, Australia in May 1928?

(14) What type of aircraft did Spain's Juan de la Cierva invent?

(15) Which air race was the background to the 1965 film *Those Magnificent Men In Their Flying Machines*?

(16) Which Fred Astaire–Ginger Rogers film had a finale in which the chorus girls danced on the wings of flying aeroplanes?

(17) Which French aviator constructed this aircraft?   ▷

(18) Under the flag of which nation did the world's first supersonic transport aircraft fly?

(19) Who piloted the Hughes H4 Hercules, the largest aeroplane ever flown, when it made its one flight in November 1947?

(20) Which swing-wing combat aircraft has been developed by Britain, West Germany and Italy?

(21) Which European airline was the first to begin night passenger services?

(22) What was the destination of the first French Concorde to take off on a passenger service in January 1976?

(23) How many Sea Harriers were lost in air-to-air combat during the Falkland's Campaign?

(24) What was the name of the B-29 Superfortress which dropped the atomic bomb on Hiroshima?

(25) Which revolution brought a stop to these airborne experiments?   ▷

1. Which sport features jammers breaking out of the pack?

2. What metal are the darts preferred by professionals made of?

3. Which game does the Italian game bocci resemble?

4. How many bulls are killed in a formal bullfight?

5. From which sport has the word 'foible' been adopted into more general use?

6. Which non-mechanical sport achieves the highest speed?

7. How many bowling pins face you if you've left a 'bread line'?

8. In which sport might you tick-tack or walk the dog?

9. Which sportsmen are divided into naturals and goofy foots?

10. Which game derives its name from the Persian word *shah*, meaning a king or ruler?

11. Which martial art was developed by an Indian monk named Daruma?

12. Which part of the anatomy has been proved to be larger in Tour de France cyclists than in any other athletes?

▽

(13) What soaring target did George Ligowsky invent for marksmen?

(14) This is one of the world's most famous cricket fans. What is his name? ▷

(15) Which blood sport features a movement called a veronica?

(16) What are A.C. Milan, Ajax and Real Madrid?

(17) Which sport features snatches and clean jerks?

(18) What is a good mudder likely to win?

(19) What prompted the cancellation of the scheduled 1980 Canada Cup hockey tournament?

(20) Which Japanese sport's name is translated into English as 'the gentle game'?

(21) Which sport are these people competing in? ▷

(22) What is the WBC?

(23) Which target sport requires about 40 acres for an international competition?

(24) Which European race sees the winner of its mountain stage awarded a jersey with large red polka dots?

(25) What colour is the five point ring on an archery target?

(1) Which island separates the Canadian part of the Niagara Falls from the American part?

(2) On which Aegean island was the Venus de Milo found in 1820?
▽

(3) If you lived in Tristan da Cunha where would your nearest neighbours, outside the island group, be?

(4) On which island was this bird hunted to extinction?
▽

(5) Where are the islands of Langerhans?

(6) On which Mediterranean island would you find this, Europe's highest volcano?
▽

(7) Which island group became the final resting place of the author of *Treasure Island*?

(8) What tropic line passes through Taiwan?

(9) For how many years were the New Territories of Hong Kong leased to Britain in 1898?

(10) Haiti and the Dominican Republic share which Caribbean island?

(11) What was the home town of Johann Wyss's Swiss Family Robinson?

(12) Which is Europe's largest island?

(13) By what other name are the Islas Malvinas also commonly known?

(14) The flag of Hawaii carries the flag of which nation in its upper left-hand corner?

△

(15) Which of Mendelssohn's compositions was particularly inspired by this view?

(16) Which French post-Impressionist painter died in the Marquesas islands in 1903?

(17) On which island is this knight buried?

▽

(18) What former penal colony lies off the coast of French Guiana?

(19) The adventures of the Scots sailor Alexander Selkirk are supposed to have inspired the story named after which island inhabitant?

(20) The flag of which nation flies over Easter island?

(21) Which group of Pacific islands did Captain James Cook name the Sandwich Islands?

(22) Who was the Jersey Lily?

(23) Which group of islands carry the Danish name that means 'Sheep Islands' in English?

▽

△

(24) Who is this man, who served as Governor and Commander-in-Chief of the Bahama Islands from 1940 until the end of World War II?

(25) Which Mediterranean island was celebrated in antiquity for its copper mines?

1   Who had hits with *Save the Last Dance for Me* and *Under the Boardwalk* in the sixties?

2   What band did this man lead?
    ▽

8   Which Jane Fonda film inspired this band's name?
    ▽

3   Which band did this boy spring to fame with?   ▷

4   Who is the most successful living songwriter in British chart history?

5   Who was the oldest member of The Beatles?

6   Who was lead singer and founder of the Doors?

7   What was the surname of 'Mama' Cass of the Mamas and the Papas?

(9) What was the name of the Velvet Underground's female vocalist?

(10) Which writer and singer made his acting debut in *Pat Garrett and Billy the Kid* in 1973?

△

(11) Which band's lead singer is shown here?

(12) How much, in dollars, were Alice Cooper's babies worth in 1973?

(13) Which producer was famed for his work with the Shirells and the Ronettes?

(14) Mickey Dolenz, Michael Nesmith, Davy Jones – who is ▷ the missing Monkee?

(15) Which film introduced the song *The First Time Ever I Saw Your Face*?

(16) Which American group did the Wilson brothers form in 1961?

(17) What kind of apple is on The Beatles' Apple label?

(18) What links a London station, a battlefield and Abba's Eurovision hit?

(19) By what name is John Deutschendorf better known?

(20) Who played drums on *Roxanne* by Police?

(21) What's the best-selling record album of all time?

(22) Who invited everyone to do The Twist?

(23) Who is Carly Simon said to have had in mind when she wrote *You're So Vain*?

(24) Which Detroit-based record company was founded by Berry Gordy Jnr.?

(25) Which famous Frank Sinatra record stayed in the charts for a record 127 weeks?

1. What is the date of Twelfth Night?

2. Which saint's feast day is celebrated on 6 December?

3. What important event in American history is remembered on 17 September?

4. The shooting season for this bird begins on 12 August in Britain. What is the bird?
▽

5. Which of Shakespeare's heroines was born on Lammas Eve?

6. Which significant anniversary in American history was President Calvin Coolidge's birthday?

7. Which English king is particularly remembered on 29 May, Oak Apple Day?

8. The first day of which month is St David's Day?

9. Who wrote the poem *The Eve of St Agnes*?

10. On which day of the year are these ladies traditionally thought to fly? ▷

11. What night precedes May Day?

12. Which saint, closely associated with the weather, is remembered on 15 July?

13. Which day is Scotland's national day?

14. When does a large Irish parade take place in New York City each year?

15. When is Labour Day celebrated in the Communist world?

16. On the last day of which month did Samuel Pepys end his diary in 1669?

(17) In what month does this Princess celebrate her wedding anniversary?

▽

(24) Who is this composer, who celebrated his tricentenary in 1985?

△

(25) Exactly how many years separate the day that the first man flew in space and the day Confederate guns fired on Fort Sumter starting the American Civil War?

(18) On what date was an atomic bomb dropped on Nagasaki?

(19) In a single year the first wife of an English king died, his second wife was executed and he married his third. Who was he?

(20) Which 20th-century American president shares the same birthday as the People's Republic of China?

(21) What is this event, celebrated each year on the 14 July ▷ by the people of France?

(22) The second oldest republic in the Americas celebrates its independence every New Year's Day. Which country is it?

(23) Which saint's day in 1929 marked the end of the road for seven of Bugs Moran's gang in Chicago?

1 Which of Shakespeare's plays is about the English king known as 'The Boar'?

2 What is the title of the Hitchcock film which was made from the book *The Wheel Spins* by Ethel Lina White?
▽

3 What was French novelist Amandine Aurore Lucie Dupin better known as?

4 Which best-seller was originally titled *Ba! Ba! Black Sheep*?

5 Who, in a novel by Oscar Wilde, remains young while his portrait ages?

6 Whose second book, published in 1965, was titled *A Spaniard in the Works*?

7 Which monthly magazine is subtitled *The International Magazine for Men*?

8 What was the *African Queen* of C. S. Forrester's novel?

9 Who described her pupils as '*la crème de la crème*'?

10 Which of Shakespeare's characters is referred to simply as 'Egypt'?

11 Which artist had the surname Buonarroti?

12 Which Jane Austen novel was originally titled *First Impressions*?

13 Which Queen is most closely associated with detective stories?

14 Which Shakespeare play has the alternative title, *What You Will*?

15 Who wrote *The Novels of Aphra Benn*?

16 What is the name of this man, who kept the most famous diary in the English language?
▽

△

(17) Who is known as 'The Father of Western Philosophy'?

(18) What was the name of this fairy?

▽

△

(19) What is the title of the film which was made from the book *The Small Woman* by Alan Burgess?

(20) What was the name of the hypnotic magician in George du Maurier's *Trilby*?

(21) Which brothers wrote *Snow White and the Seven Dwarfs*?

(22) What was Eric Blair's pen name?

(23) Who painted *Soft Self-Portrait with Grilled Bacon*?

(24) What name did Napoleon Bonaparte sign to his letters?

(25) Whose biography is titled *Groucho and Me*?

(1) How many tines are there on a standard dinner fork?

(2) What is 'room temperature' in degrees Fahrenheit?

(3) How many are there in a standard book of matches?

(4) What is the great and proud claim to fame of Thomas Crapper?

(5) What did Ellen and Ebenezer Butterick invent and first sell in 1863?

(6) What puts the fizz in soda water?

(7) Which is more tender, the left or right leg of a chicken?

(8) How many drops make a dash in cooking?

(9) Whose army were canned foods developed to feed?

(10) How many teaspoons are there in a tablespoon?

(11) What do dilute acetic acid and vegetable oil make?

(12) What country did Venetian blinds originate in?

(13) What unit of heat will raise the temperature of one gram of water by one degree Celsius?

(14) What is this contraption?
▽

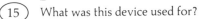

(15) What was this device used for?

(16) What is the mythical Otto Titzling credited with inventing?

(17) What was first marketed as Gayetty's Medicated Paper?

(18) Who patented the first of these?

(19) Who was the Frenchman credited with the invention of this machine?

(20) Who patented a carpet sweeper in 1876?

(21) In which Shakespeare play is there a recipe which includes eye of newt, toe of frog, wool of bat and tongue of dog?

(22) With which form of home entertainment is the name of John Logie Baird connected?

(23) What does the camera shutter speed B stand for?

(24) What is the name given to what is generally thought to be the earliest form of domestic can opener?

(25) Which prolific American inventor is said to have invented the safety-pin in 1849 to pay off a small debt?

1. In which Australian state was the official world water speed record set in October 1978?

2. Which yacht did Ted Turner captain to victory in the 1977 America's Cup championship?

3. Which European body of water was Matthew Webb the first to swim in 1875?

4. What does the starter say to rowing crews when he wants the race to start?

5. Which Olympic swimming races start in the water?

6. How many people are there in one of the boats participating in the Oxford and Cambridge Boat Race?

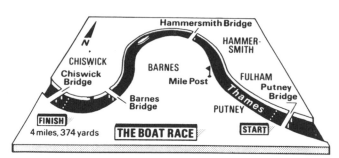

Hammersmith Bridge
HAMMERSMITH
CHISWICK
Chiswick Bridge
BARNES
Mile Post
FULHAM
Putney Bridge
Barnes Bridge
PUTNEY
Thames
FINISH
4 miles, 374 yards
THE BOAT RACE
START

7. Does a yachtsman's 'fresh breeze' mean a velocity of?
a) 10 knots   b) 15 knots   c) 20 knots?

8. Which swimming style was officially separated from an existing one in 1952 to become a technique in its own right?

9. Which country does the international yachting designation KC signify?

10. How many members of a water polo team play at any one time?

11. Which swimming stroke did this man use in competing for Harvard?

12. Which has the taller mizzenmast – a ketch or a yawl?

13. What do the water-loving competitors in Australia's Moomba Masters put on their feet?

14. What does the sub-aqua acronym Scuba stand for?

15. What is a swimming pool that measures 164 ft by 68 ft 11 in (50 m by 21 m) better known as?

16. Which European country is home to the world's oldest yacht club?

17. Which British prime minister raced this yacht?
▽

(18) For which piece of watersport equipment did the American Fred Walter file a patent in the early 1920s?

(19) Which Australian city became the home of the America s Cup?

◁ (20) In which sport are these girls participating?

(21) What's a natatorium?

(22) What fish did Alfred Dean catch in Ceduna, Australia on 21 April 1959 to establish a saltwater All-Tackle fishing record?

△

(23) Which 1930s Olympic freestyle champion starred in the Buck Rogers and Flash Gordon serials?

(24) On which European river have the longest record rides on a river bore been set?

◁ (25) In which Olympic watersport were the father and brother of this star both medal winners?

(1) Which group of stars are depicted on the Australian flag?

(2) Which European explorer was the first to discover New Zealand on his voyage of 1642?

(3) What part of Antarctica is administered by New Zealand?

(4) What was originally called Van Diemen's Land?

(5) What natural breakwater lies off the northeast coast of Australia?

(6) What was the title of the 1960 movie set in Australia and starring Deborah Kerr, Robert Mitchum and Peter Ustinov?

(7) Which Australian city became home to the America's Cup?

(8) Which town in South Australia became the home of the Long Range Weapons Establishment in 1946?

(9) In which year did this activity first catch on in Australia and develop into a rush?
a) 1849 b) 1851 c) 1861

△
(10) Which Australian outlaw did this artist portray in a 1969 movie?

(11) What is this musical instrument called?
▽

(12) On which of New Zealand's islands is the country's capital?

(13) Who is the man behind this famous lady?   ▷

(14) Which Australian city was named after the father of the theory of evolution?

(15) Which American architect designed Canberra?

(16) What large flat area of Australia has a name which means 'no tree' in Latin?

(17) Which Australian prime minister disappeared while swimming?

(18) What famous Sydney landmark was opened on 19 March 1932?

(19) What did about three hundred police and soldiers attack near Ballarat, Victoria in 1854?

(20) Do more New Zealanders live on the North or South Island?

(21) Which bird is on Australia's coat of arms?

ADVANCE AUSTRALIA

(22) What fruit has a name in common with a New Zealand bird?

(23) Which Australian starred with John Travolta in the movie *Grease*?

(24) What famous Australian landmark is this?   ▷

(25) Which Australian city is served by Tullamarine airport?

(1) What was the title of the 1969 Broadway musical about the framing of the Declaration of Independence?

(2) Which Broadway musical was based on T.H. White's novel *The Once and Future King*?

(3) Which musical is set in Catfish Row?

(4) Which 1953 Broadway musical introduced the song *Stranger in Paradise*?

(5) Which 'horror' won the award for best musical of the year in 1973?

(6) Which theatre company is responsible for this wildly successful show?

▽

(7) Who starred with Woody Allen in the stage version of *Play It Again Sam*?

(8) In which play did Elizabeth Taylor score a triumph on Broadway in 1981 and in London's West End a year later?

(9) Which Broadway hit, later turned into a successful film in 1978, ran for 3388 performances in New York?

(10) During rehearsals for which 1980s musical was this photograph taken?

▽

(11) Which 'mammoth' 1980 Broadway success gave David Bowie his stage debut?

(12) Which 1967 rock musical had 1750 Broadway performances and grossed $80 million worldwide?

▵

(13) What's so special about this actor's appearance in the musical *Time*?

(14) Which actor starred in both the stage and film productions of *Cabaret*?

(15) On what play was *Oklahoma!* based?

(16) Which musical by Tim Rice and Andrew Lloyd Webber followed *Jesus Christ Superstar*?

(17) Which 1960 musical, set in England, introduced the song *I Wonder What The King Is Doing Tonight*?

(18) Which American writer was depicted in the musical *White Suit Blues*?

(19) Which 1960 musical was centred on this rock star? ▷

(20) Which 1956 musical hit was described by Brooks Atkinson's comment, 'it may be the only musical in which the hero and heroine never kiss or embrace'?

(21) Which Broadway smash hit had Laurence Olivier and Anthony Quinn switching roles as Henry II and Thomas à Becket to freshen the show?

(22) Who wrote *A Funny Thing Happened on the Way to the Forum*?

(23) Who was the author of the first musical to win a Pulitzer Prize for drama, in 1932?

▵

(24) Which 1986 musical is this Abba-dominated team responsible for?

(25) Which 1972 musical saw David Essex as Jesus Christ?

1. What did Abolitionists try to end?

2. Which US statesman said, 'This generation of Americans has a rendezvous with destiny'?

3. What's the only house in England that the Queen may not enter?

4. What class is categorised as the bourgeoisie?

5. What city has the world's largest black population?

6. What disease plagued Europe, Africa and Asia in the fourteenth century?

7. What did Englishman John Hawkins begin selling to New World colonists in 1562?

8. In which South African town were seventy blacks killed in a 'massacre' in the 60 s?

9. Which country's people were most heavily bombed during the Vietnam war?

10. Which international children's charity received all of Rod Stewart's royalties from *Do You Think I'm Sexy*?

11. Who founded this popular army?

△

12. Which American composer wrote the *Fanfare For The Common Man* in 1942?

13. In which play by Robert Bolt does the Common Man act as the commentator?

14. Who collaborated with Karl Marx in writing *The Communist Manifesto*?

15. Which country was the first to have universal suffrage?

16. Who was the commander of Italy's 'Red Shirts'?

17. Which shop started out with the slogan, 'Don't ask the price – it's a penny'?

18. Which three words proclaimed the French Revolution?
▽

19. In which Alabama city was Mrs Rosa Parks arrested for sitting down in one of the front seats of a city bus?

20. To which school did President Eisenhower send five hundred troops from the 101 Airborne Division on 24 September, 1957?

21. Who was king of England at the time of the Peasants' Revolt?

22. Which war was immediately followed by a violent uprising in Paris known as the *Commune*?

23. What was the name given to the only republican period in English history?

24. Which charter establishing eight fundamental principles for national and personal liberty was declared by Roosevelt and Churchill in August 1941?

25. Why did this man miss the first Communist Party Congress in London?
▽

1. Which French sculptor is responsible for *The Kiss*? ▷

2. Which city is graced by Michelangelo's *David*?

3. What did Thomas Sheraton design and produce?

4. Which literary character is represented by a sculpture in London's Kensington Gardens?

5. What is missing from the Venus de Milo?

6. Which wood is Chippendale furniture made from?

7. Which Michelangelo statue was 'hammered' into the headlines by fanatic Laszlo Toth in May 1972?

8. Which French engineer built a tower for the 1889 Paris Exposition?

9. Which sculptor's work is this? ▽

10. Which Swiss architect was engaged to design the new capital of the Punjab, Chandigargh?

11. In what familiar Parisian settings can examples of Hector Guimard's wrought iron work still be seen?

12. Which great architect designed St Paul's Cathedral in London?

13. Who was the Florentine sculptor who became well known for his autobiography, written between 1558 and 1562?

14. What kind of things did Capability Brown design?

15. Who founded the Habitat design empire?

16. Which famous American landmark was designed by F. A. Bartholdi?

△

(17) Who designed this car?

(18) In which English seaside town can you see this pavilion, designed by John Nash?
▽

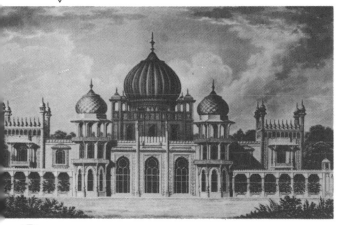

(19) Who was the 'founder of modern sculpture' whose famous bronze *David* stands today in Florence's Bargello Museum?

(20) Which great English architect was also engaged by the court of James I to design scenery for masques and plays?

(21) What in Picasso's sculpture *Bull's Head* did he employ to create the horns?

(22) Who modelled the bronze lions at the foot of Nelson's column in Trafalgar Square?

(23) Who played Michelangelo in the 1965 film *The Agony and the Ecstasy*?

(24) Which English pottery house is famous for designs like these? ▽

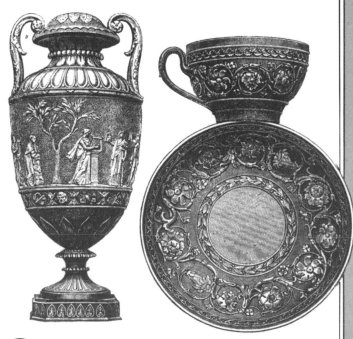

(25) Of which German design movement was this the symbol?

(1) What automobile was known as the Flying Teapot?

(2) What was the nickname of the Model T Ford?

▽

(3) What is the voltage of most car batteries?

(4) What day of the week sees the most fatal car accidents?

(5) Which cities were the start and finish of the first intercontinental auto race in 1908?

(6) Where does a car with the letters CH come from?

(7) What meter was invented by C. C. Magee in 1935?

(8) Which rock and roll singer was killed in a motor accident on Easter Day 1960?

(9) Which car manufacturer traditionally said, 'You can have it any colour so long as it is black'?

(10) In which 1964 movie did number 24 in this picture drive a gadget-filled Aston Martin?

▽

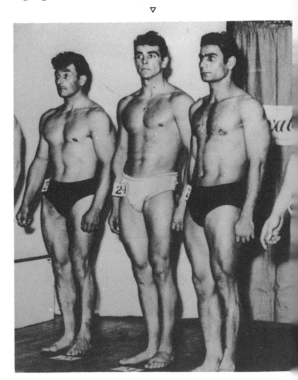

(11) What make was the Presidential car delivered to the American Secret Service in October 1968?

(12) Which of the world's capitals has the largest taxi fleet?

(13) Which British car originally sold for £496 19s 2d in August 1959?

△

(14) Who designed this car?

(15) What colour flag had to be carried in front of mechanically propelled vehicles, according to Britain's 1865 Locomotives Act?

(16) Which of these would you find in a petrol engine but *not* in a diesel engine?
a) dynamo   b) oil pump   c) carburettor

(17) What was the name of this car, star of a 1953 movie?   ▷

(18) What title did the car manufacturer William Richard Morris take in 1934?

(19) What do wet Formula 1 tyres have that dry ones don't?

(20) Which Italian city is referred to by the 'T' in FIAT?

(21) What colour were the original entwined 'Rs' in the Rolls-Royce emblem?

(22) How was the first road vehicle to exceed 60 mph (96.5 km/h) powered?

(23) What became mandatory equipment on American cars on 1 March 1968?

(24) Who was the inventor of this ill-fated form of transport?   ▷

(25) Which celebrity died when her scarf caught in the rear wheel of a friend's car in Nice on 14 September 1927?

△

1. What is the most popular spectator sport in America?

2. Who was the first Commissioner of Baseball?

3. How many seconds must a cowboy stay aboard a rodeo bronc?

4. How tall does a basketball player have to be to qualify as a septipedalian?

5. Which stadium do the Miami Dolphins play their home games in?

6. Which Kennedy scored Harvard's only touchdown in a 21–7 loss to Yale in 1955?

7. Which two English games was this sport derived from?
   ▽

8. Which team did Bob Cousy help to six NBA championships?

9. What is the most common nickname of American college football teams?

10. Which of baseball's major leagues evolved from the Western Association?

11. Whose home run won the first major league baseball All-Star Game?

12. In which American state was this sport first formalized?
    ▽

13. Which player on a basketball team usually plays the post, or pivot, position?

14. Which NFL team do the Embraceable Ewes cheer for?

15. Which New York Yankee catcher was killed in a plane crash on 2 August 1979?

16. Which zone varies from batter to batter in baseball?

17. Which city's baseball park boasts the world's largest beer barrel?

18. Which sport is known as 'The Grand Old Game'?

19. Which is the oldest of the Bowl games played in American College Football?

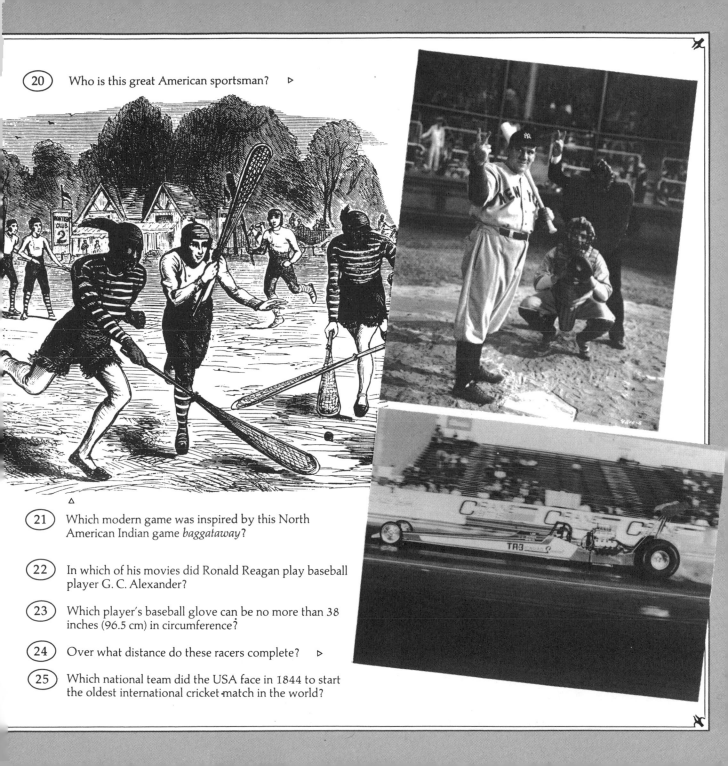

20 Who is this great American sportsman? ▷

△

21 Which modern game was inspired by this North American Indian game *baggataway*?

22 In which of his movies did Ronald Reagan play baseball player G. C. Alexander?

23 Which player's baseball glove can be no more than 38 inches (96.5 cm) in circumference?

24 Over what distance do these racers complete? ▷

25 Which national team did the USA face in 1844 to start the oldest international cricket match in the world?

1 Which are the only two perennial vegetables?

2 What crop is grown in these fields?
   ▽

3 Which fruit has the most calories?

4 What are these creatures traditionally used to hunt for?
   ▽

5 What is the most extensively grown and eaten food?

6 What is the oldest known vegetable?

7 What is the largest American agricultural crop by weight?

8 What is the syrup drained from raw sugar called?

9 What were broccoli and cauliflower developed from?

10 What is the common name of the vegetable *Beta vulgaris*?

11 What colour is a Granny Smith apple?

12 If farming is agriculture, what kind of 'culture' is being practised by the people who grow this crop?
    ▽

13 Which vegetable yields the most pounds of produce per acre?

14 What is the most popular beverage in the USA?

15 Which country has the world's largest sheep population?

16. What crop failure caused the Irish Famine?

◁ 17. Which crop is traditionally dried in this kind of building?

18. What colour is yak's milk?

19. What form of agriculture did Moses practise before he was called by God?

20. What famous farming family lives in Ambridge?

21. On which island is the world's most southerly vineyard?

22. Which actress played the luxury-loving wife moved out to *Green Acres* by her lawyer husband in the 1965–70 TV series?

23. Which is the most rural state in the USA?

24. Which country has the world's largest wild rice farm?

25. Which animal was domesticated first ?
a) the sheep b) the cow c) the pig

(1) Who played Noel Coward in the movie *Star!*?

(2) Which American comedian's autobiography is titled *How To Talk Dirty and Influence People*?

(3) Who was the coalminer's son who shattered all the performance attendance records in Las Vegas in 1969?

(4) What's the nickname of the owner of this famous nose?

▽

(5) Whose name ended the graffiti, 'To do is to be – John Stuart Mill; To be is to do – Jean-Paul Sartre; Do be, do be do ...'?

(6) Who wrote the play *The Entertainer*?

(7) Who, when asked what his golf handicap was, replied, 'I'm a one-eyed, Jewish negro'?

(8) What was the circus name of Nikolai Poliakov, who died in September 1974?

(9) Who was America's Poet Lariat who once commented, 'There's no such thing as a big rope trick, rope tricks is all little'?

(10) Which club had its stage sawn up and sold in pieces after its closure in 1966?

(11) Which American entertainer said in a 1978 interview, 'Look, I'd go out with women my age, but there are no women my age'?

(12) Who is the man who created this entertainer and his friends?

▽

(13) Which British entertainer invented Sid Snot?

(14) Which entertainer was played by Barbra Streisand in *Funny Girl*?

(15) Which famous foursome achieved their first small success playing in Texas under the name *The Six Mascots*?

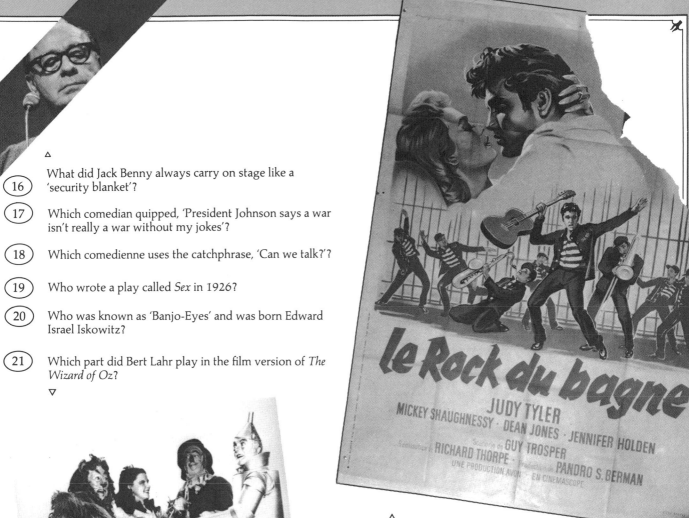

16. What did Jack Benny always carry on stage like a 'security blanket'?

17. Which comedian quipped, 'President Johnson says a war isn't really a war without my jokes'?

18. Which comedienne uses the catchphrase, 'Can we talk?'?

19. Who wrote a play called *Sex* in 1926?

20. Who was known as 'Banjo-Eyes' and was born Edward Israel Iskowitz?

21. Which part did Bert Lahr play in the film version of *The Wizard of Oz*?

22. What year did this man die?

23. Which entertainer was appointed Toastmaster General of the US by President Truman?

24. Which famous pianist was once described as the 'Danny Kaye of comedy'?

25. Who was the 'sock it to me' girl on *Laugh-In*?

1. Who was the first Catholic president of the USA?

2. What future British prime minister's only novel was *Savrola*?

3. Which South African statesman was portrayed in the film *Gandhi* by the playwright Athol Fugard?

4. Which city was Benigno Aquino assassinated in on 21 August 1983?

5. After which American president is the capital of Liberia named?

6. Which World War II leader allegedly fathered a daughter named Uschi?

7. Which subject did Joseph Stalin study for five years in Tiflis, Georgia from 1894 to 1899?

8. Which president peers from Mount Rushmore on Theodore Roosevelt's immediate left?

▽

△

9. Who lies buried under the dome of this Parisian building?

10. What kind of plane was American president Lyndon Johnson sworn in on?

11. Which European statesman's book *The Prince* was condemned by Pope Clement VIII?

12. Which American secretary of state once noted, 'I go out with actresses because I'm not apt to marry one'?

13. In what country was Russian revolutionary Leon Trotsky assassinated?

14. Who founded the Jewish Documentation Center?

15. Of which African country was Daniel arap Moi elected president?

16. Which ship received a naval escort after Muammar Qadaffi threatened to torpedo it in 1973?

△

(17) Which of these 'Nazis' became Governor of California?
a) b) c)

(18) What form of air transport prompted this man's resignation from the British Cabinet in 1986?

▽

(19) Which Russian leader was *Time*'s Man of the Year for 1957?

(20) Who was nicknamed Germany's 'Iron Chancellor'?

(21) Who led Egypt into the 1967 war against Israel?

(22) What significance did the number 49 have for American president James Knox Polk in 1846?

(23) Who replaced Zulfiqar Ali Bhutto as head of state in Pakistan in July 1977?

(24) How many men had been American president before Ronald Reagan?

(25) Where was Mao Tse-tung's most prominent facial wart?

1. Which adventurous cartoon character was invented by Georges Remi of Belgium?

2. What is the most common name in nursery rhymes?

3. How many years did Sleeping Beauty sleep?

4. What kind of animal was Pinocchio's pet Figaro?

5. Which city is patrolled by Batman and Robin?

6. Which nursery rhyme character was warned that the cow was in the corn?

7. What is this bear's favourite snack?
▽

8. What is the name of the giant who swallows Tom Thumb?

9. Who created this bear?　　　　▷

10. Which character in *Wind in the Willows* declared that there was nothing, 'half so much worth doing as simply messing about in boats'?

11. What was Charles Dodgson's profession, when he wasn't concerned with wonderlands and looking-glasses?

12. What does Beauty ask her father to bring her on his return in the story of *Beauty and the Beast*?

13. In which present-day country is the setting of the story of *The Pied Piper of Hamelin*?

14. What is the surname of the three children, Wendy, John and Michael in the story of *Peter Pan*?
▽

(15) Who is this character who owned the chocolate factory in the film of Roald Dahl's story?

▽

(21) Which author wrote *Swallows and Amazons*, *Winter Holiday* and *Secret Water*?

(22) Who was the writer who created Mary Poppins?

(23) Which fairy story was turned into the 1976 movie *The Slipper and the Rose*?

(24) What was Miss Muffet eating when the spider joined her?

(25) What name did Rudyard Kipling give to this character in *The Jungle Book*?

▽

(16) What did the Owl and the Pussycat go to sea in?

(17) Who created Prince Caspian and Aslan?

(18) Which guest is pushed head first into the teapot in *Alice's Adventures in Wonderland*?

(19) Which of the Seven Dwarfs comes first alphabetically? ▷

(20) What do Tiggers do best?

(1) Which ocean liner was retired in 1967 to become a hotel at Long Beach?

△

(2) How do you send the signal 'SOS' in the international code invented by this man?

(3) How deep is 'mark twain'?

(4) How many masts does a sloop have?

(5) How many compass point names are there?

(6) What is the name of this French marine scientist's research ship?

▽

(7) Which ship was found mysteriously abandoned four weeks after leaving Boston bound for Genoa in November 1872?

(8) What colour is the light displayed on the starboard side of a ship?

(9) Which ship collided with the Swedish liner *Stockholm* on 26 July 1956?

(10) What was the name of Germany's largest World War II battleship?

(11) What does a compass needle point to?

(12) What do you call a boy born between cannons on a British warship?

(13) What was the name of the ship in which Columbus made his first Atlantic crossing?

(14) What was the name of the first vessel designed to winter in the polar pack ice?

△

(15) Who starred as Captain Queeg in this 1954 movie?

(16) How much fuel did the USS *Nautilus*, the world's first nuclear powered-submarine, use in her first ten years of service?
a) 12 lbs (5 kg) b) 120 lbs (50 kg) c) 1200 lbs (500 kg)

(17) What is a stay on board a ship?

(18) What did the American submarine *Triton* achieve on 10 May 1960?

(19) What was the name of the first ship to be propelled by steam turbines?

(20) Which ship held the Blue Riband of the North Atlantic for the longest period?

(21) Which was the first American naval vessel to be captured at sea since the war of 1812?

(22) What nationality was the first warship sunk by surface-to-surface guided missiles?

(23) Down which Asian river did HMS *Amethyst* make her historic escape in 1949?

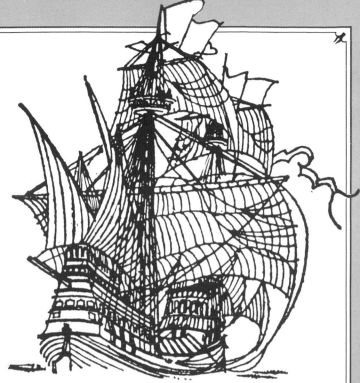

(24) What is the name of the great warship which sank off Portsmouth, England, in July 1545?

(25) What was the name of this, the last naval battle fought between galleys manned by oarsmen?

▽

1. For which popular card game did Edmond Hoyle codify the rules in 1742?

2. Which game is known in various countries as blind fly, blind cow and blind buck?

3. What was this originally called?　▷　▷　▷　▷　▷

4. What is the point value of the outer bullseye on a dartboard?

5. How many sticks are used in jackstraws or pickup sticks?

6. Which playing card is the symbol of love?

7. How many properties are there on a Monopoly board?

8. How many decks of cards are generally used to keep a contract bridge game flowing?

9. How many different colours are the spaces on a Scrabble board?

10. What game can you crown your men in?

11. What is the bonus for going gin in gin rummy?

12. Which two colours of stones are used in Go?

13. What did Minh Tai solve in 26 seconds in a December 1981 competition?

14. What kind of game was Nolan Bushnell the first to invent?

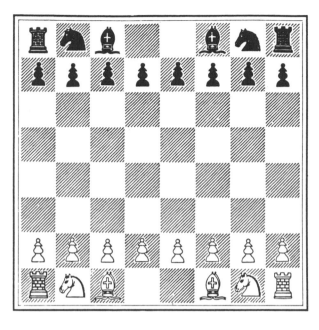

21. What do you mean when you tug your earlobe in Charades?

22. Which oriental game comprises of 144 tiles?

23. What category does the colour pink denote in Trivial Pursuit's Baby Boomer edition?

24. Which game's board shows the territories of Irkutsk, Yakutsk and Kamchatka?

25. Which way does the jack of hearts normally face?

▽

△

15. What colour square does the white king start a chess game on?

16. What is the British game of noughts and crosses properly called in North America?

17. How many strikes does each player get per turn in conkers

18. What are skipped in the pastime once known as Ducks and Drakes?

19. In which country did the yo-yo originate as a hunting weapon?

20. What popular children's optical toy was devised by Sir David Brewster in 1816?

1. Which international organization was established in Addis Ababa in 1963?

2. How did this man cause an adjournment of the 25th anniversary session of the UN General Assembly?

▽

△

9. Which international criminal organization did this secret agent encounter on many of his assignments?

10. Which three countries signed the Anzus Treaty in 1951?

11. Where did the League of Nations establish its Permanent Court of International Justice?

12. In which country did this man organize his 26th of July Movement?

▽

3. What nationality was the first secretary-general of the United Nations?

4. What does OAS stand for?

5. In which year was NATO formed?
a) 1947   b) 1949   c) 1952

6. What is the Moslem equivalent of the Red Cross?

7. In which of the world's capitals does Interpol have its headquarters?

8. Who is the idol of the German Organization of Non-Commercial Supporters of Donaldism?

△

13) Who is this man, who was the secretary-general of the United Nations during the 1962 Cuban missile crisis?

14) Britain, China, the Soviet Union and America are four permanent members of the United Nations Security Council – which country is the fifth?

15) Which two South American countries are members of OPEC?

16) Which country's entire population was condemned to death by the Spanish Inquisition?

17) Which Pope called the Second Vatican Council in 1962?

18) Where does the FAO have its headquarters?

19) The Italian peninsula contains two sovereign states that are not members of the UN. San Marino is one of them, what is the other?

20) Who is the International President of the World Wildlife Fund?

21) Representatives of 147 churches from 44 countries met in Amsterdam in 1948 to inaugurate which religious organization?

22) In which US city was the American half of the Band Aid concert held in 1985?

23) What historic union occurred in 1801?

24) What Nobel Prize category is the only one awarded by Norwegians?

25) Who founded this organization in 1907?

▽

(1) Who played Grasshopper in TV's *Kung Fu*?

(2) Who shot this character?

(3) Whose story was portrayed in *The Naked Civil Servant*?

(4) What is St Eligius's Hospital better known as?

(5) Which actor swapped Sherwood Forest for the Moldavian aristocracy?

(6) Which TV series gave us 'something completely different'?

(7) Who plays Steve McGarret in *Hawaii Five-O*?

(8) In which police series does this duo star?

(9) Which British TV series inspired the American show *All in the Family*?

(10) What was the name of Dr Who's dog?

(11) What is the nickname of this *M.A.S.H.* character?

△
(12) Who played this TV character?

(13) Which TV series featured Corporal Rocco Barbella?

(14) Which TV series featured a nose-wiggling witch called Samantha?

(15) What are the names of the characters played by these stars of *Minder*?
▽

(16) What city was the setting for *Gunsmoke*?

(17) How long was the TV mission of *Star Trek* to be?

(18) Who played the lead role in *I, Claudius*?

(19) Which TV series featured Ford Prefect and Arthur Dent?

(20) What was the name of the Addams family's butler?

(21) What is the first name of this TV detective?
▷

△
(22) Who is Miss Piggy in love with?

(23) Which wondrous woman won the 1972 Miss USA title?

(24) Which *Peyton Place* star married Frank Sinatra?

(25) Who starred as a psychiatrist in TV's *The Human Jungle*?

1 What nationality is this woman, who founded The Order of the Missionaries of Charity in Calcutta in 1948.

▽

2 Who did the *New York Herald* send to look for African explorer David Livingstone?

▽

△

3 Which leader wore an unearned VC in the 1970s?

4 In which year did the South African Citizenship Act begin the *apartheid* programme?
a) 1919　b) 1929　c) 1949

5 Which country did Richard Nixon make a historic visit to on 21 February 1972?

6 Which pop star donated £350 000 to Nicaragua in 197 for its earthquake victims?

7 In which African country is Timbuktu?

8 Who became President of the first Egyptian Republic i June 1956?

9 Which country did the USA break off relations with or 3 January 1961?

(10) Who did Augustus Pinochet overthrow as President of Chile?

(11) Which Indian statesman coined the term 'The Third World'?

(12) Which African tribe did Albert Luthuli, winner of the 1960 Nobel Peace Prize, belong to?

(13) What 'kicked off' the war between El Salvador and Honduras in 1969?

(14) What did East Pakistan change its name to in 1971?

(15) In which Arab country did Idi Amin finally take refuge?

(16) What country did Pol Pot terrorize?

(17) Whose flight from Tibet was headlined in 1959?

(18) Which country did this man flee in 1986?
▽

(19) Which British statesman announced in a speech in Cape Town in 1960 'The wind of change is blowing through this continent'?

(20) Which South American country had its population reduced from 1 400 000 to only 220 000 in the 1864–70 war with its neighbours?

(21) Which Frederick Forsyth novel deals with a mercenary-backed coup in a small West African country?

(22) This is the heaviest king in the world. Of which country is he the ruler?
▽

(23) With which African country was the Frelimo independence movement associated?

(24) Which French territory in the Indian Ocean was originally known as Ile Bourbon?

(25) Which country surrounds The Gambia on all its land frontiers?

1. For paintings of the coast of which American state is Winslow Homer best known?

2. Which American architect is celebrated in a song by Simon and Garfunkel?

3. Which Americans produced this kind of art? ▷

4. The first group of American landscape painters was named after a river. Which was it?
a) The Hudson   b) The Missouri   c) The Mississippi

5. What particular art form did Alexander Calder invent?

6. Which famous engineer and communications innovator was also an accomplished painter, with works like his portrait of Lafayette in New York's City Hall?

7. Who painted the boxing picture titled *The Salute* in 1898?

8. What is the name of this famous Boston silversmith?
▽

9. Who was the cartoonist who created the beautiful, well-bred 'girl' named after him?

10. Which American painter, born in Florence, spent most of his professional life working in England where he became the most fashionable portrait painter of his age?

11) Who was the celebrated painter who replied to a lady who told him that a landscape reminded her of his work, 'Yes madam, Nature is creeping up'?

12) Which 19th-century American craftsman became famous for glass?

13) Which famous American artist painted this?

▽

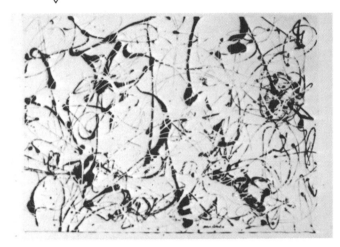

14) Who designed the geodesic domes that made up the American Pavilion at Montreal's Expo '67? ▷

15) For which 'mountainous' sculpture is Gutzon Borglum remembered?

16) Grant Wood painted the people and places of one American state in particular. Which one?

17) The architects of which South American civilization designed the Temple of the Sun at Cuzco, Peru?

18) Which American artist was shot by Valerie Soliuas?

19) To which genre of painting did the Quaker painter Edward Hicks belong?

20) Who painted western works like *Bronco Buster* and *Cavalry Charge on the Southern Plains*?

21) What were Grandma Moses's first names?

22) Which ball game is captured in one of Ben Shahn's best known works?

23) Which man invented 'rayographs'?

24) Which Pennsylvania artist, totally blind at her death, became famous for her domestic scenes, among them *The Bath*?

25) Which Chicago artist is famous for her feminist dinner party?

1. How many tentacles does a squid have?

2. What was the name of Henry Williamson's otter? ▷

3. What are walrus tusks made of?

4. Which fish's skin was once used commercially as sandpaper?

5. What sort of creature was television's Flipper?

6. What fish is served up as kippers, whitebait and bloaters?

7. What name did this man give to his fictional submarine which explored the mysteries of the deep in one of his most popular stories? ▷

8. Which resort is terrorized by sharks in this film? ▽

9. What water creature features in the title of an album by this man? ▷

10. With what would you expect to be served if you ordered *moules marinières* in a restaurant?

11. What sort of young fish is a smolt?

12. Which African water creature kills the most people?

13. What is a shark's skeleton made of?
a) bone   b) muscle   c) cartilage

14. What sea creature does a crayfish closely resemble?

15. What is a Portuguese man-of-war?

16. How many hearts does an octopus have?

17. Who created the cartoon character Captain Haddock?

18. What does a whale shark feed on?

19. What type of fish is reckoned to be the most valuable, from a culinary point of view?

20. The pilchard is an adult form of which small fish?

21. What do you call a young infant whale?

22. What is the name of this species of Indian crocodile? ▷

23. With which country did the UK have the so-called 'Cod War'?

24. What prehistoric fish, thought to have been extinct for thousands of years, was netted off the coast of southern Africa in 1938?

25. How does the archer fish catch its prey?

1. Which race did Joan Benoit win in the 1984 Summer Olympics?

2. What protective devices are all Olympic wrestlers required to wear?

3. How many Olympic Games were cancelled because of World War II?

4. What was the official 35 mm camera of the Moscow Olympics?

5. Who is this, the founder of the modern Olympic Games?
▽

6. How many continents must a game be played on to win recognition as an official Olympic sport?

7. Is a fifty-kilometre walk longer or shorter than a marathon?

8. Which Asian nation won the demonstration baseball tournament at the 1984 Summer Olympics?

9. Is the stadium for the 1936 Summer Olympics now to be found in East Berlin or West Berlin?
▽

10. What was the first African country to celebrate an Olympic gold medal?

11. What six-times Olympic champion was known as the Flying Finn?

12. How many times have the Olympic Games been held in Africa?

13. What was the official soft drink of the 1984 Summer Olympics?

14. How many musical instruments may accompany a woman gymnast's Olympic floor exercises?

15. What is the heaviest Olympic weightlifting class called?

16. Which was the first country to host the Summer and Winter Olympics in the same year?

17 Who is this figure skater, who won three Olympic gold ▷ medals?

18 How many athletes did Puerto Rico enter in the 1984 Winter Olympics?

19 Which year were pistols first used in Olympic shooting events?

20 What is the smallest city to have hosted the Summer Olympics?

21 Which member of The Rolling Stones donated $45 000 to help send the British gymnastics team to the 1984 Summer Olympics?

22 What were planted in sterilized soil and presented to athletes and officials at the Montreal Olympics?

△

23 In what sport did this film star compete at the Olympics?

24 Which member of the British royal family competed in the 1976 Summer Olympics?

25 What was the name of this symbol and mascot of the ▷ 1980 Olympic Games?

(1) Which European city has become famous for its 'gnomes'?

(2) What is the only kind of insurance not undertaken by the Corporation of Lloyd's?

(3) Which unit of currency will buy you dinner in Iraq, Jordan, Tunisia and Yugoslavia?

(4) Which country has 100 leptas to the drachma?

(5) What was Uncle Sam's biggest real estate deal?

(6) Which country's currency is considered the most difficult to counterfeit?

(7) Where can you buy a cup of coffee with cruzeiros?

(8) Which Central American country's currency shares its name with a beautiful bird from the same region.?
▽

(9) From which country did the pirates' 'pieces of eight' originate?

(10) What is the income tax rate in Kuwait?

(11) Which of the world's industrial countries has had the largest balance of payments surplus?

(12) What was the financial-sounding hit that this band enjoyed in 1976?
▽

(13) Which Middle East country has the highest per capita national wealth in the world?

(14) In which American state is the United States Bullion Depository at Fort Knox?

(15) Which South American country had an inflation rate of over 1000 per cent in 1985?

(16) Which country printed the world's first paper money?

(17) Who was this famous millionaire?

(18) Which South American country became the first nation to receive American foreign aid in 1812?

(19) Which European country was the victim of the world's worst inflation in 1946?

(20) The estate of which American multi-millionaire received the highest personal tax demand ever recorded?

(21) Which nation paid history's highest ransom for the return of its king in the 16th century?

(22) In which film does this actress sing the line, 'Money makes the world go around'?

(23) Which is the world's deepest gold mine?

(24) Which African country was once known as the Gold Coast?

(25) What, according to the Beatles, can't money buy?

1. Which play opened in London on 25 November 1952 and has been going strong ever since?

2. Who wrote *Fool For Love*?

3. Which drug was Mary Tyrone hooked on in Eugene O'Neill's play *Long Day's Journey Into Night*?

4. Who wrote *Death of a Salesman* in six weeks?

5. Which playwright's works include *The Collection* and *The Caretaker*?

6. Which Irish-born playwright was sentenced to two years hard labour for homosexuality?

7. Which Edward Albee play centres on George and Martha, a childless couple?

8. For the film version of which play did this actress win an Oscar in 1951?
▽

9. Which Peter Shaffer play is about a boy who blinds six horses?

10. Which religious figure wrote the play *The Jeweller's Shop*?

11. With which playwright has this actress been most closely associated in the last few years?
▽

12. Which Irish playwright wrote the 1959 play *The Hostage*?

13. What is the complete title of Athol Fugard's play which begins *Statements After an Arrest ...*?

14. Who are Vladimir and Estragon waiting for?

15. In which play is Lydia Languish courted by Jack Absolute?

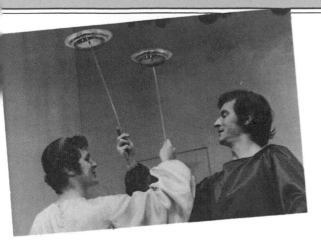

△

(16) Which play, directed by Peter Brook, was performed in this innovative white box?

(17) Which co-founder of the Group Theatre included *Waiting for Lefty* and *Till The Day I Die* among his plays?

(18) What is the name given to this kind of Japanese theatre?
▽

(19) Which English playwright had five plays running simultaneously in London's West End in 1975?

(20) Which American playwright achieved a start on Broadway with *Come Blow Your Horn* in 1961?

(21) What school of acting was founded by Lee Strasberg?

(22) By what two names are *all* of the members of a family discussed in Ionesco's *The Bald Prima Donna* known?

(23) Who was Mozart's great rival in *Amadeus*?

(24) Which playwright once observed, 'Everyone but Somerset Maugham said I was a second Somerset Maugham'?

(25) Which part did this actor once describe as not being, 'a role that an actor should ever be asked to portray for a hundred performances on end'?
▽

(1) If Christianity as a whole represents the world's largest religion (measured by numbers), which comes second?

(2) Who declared, 'I have a dream'?

(3) In which holy city is the building called the Kaaba?

(4) Of which philosophical school were these French writers important members?
▽

(5) What number did Adolf Hitler believe possessed supernatural powers?

1234567890?

(6) In which present-day country was Erasmus born?

(7) Which American president observed, 'It's a recession when your neighbour loses his job: it's a depression when you lose yours'?

(8) Who called religion the opium of the people?

(9) Who launched the Great Proletarian Cultural Revolution?

(10) What religious movement did Joseph Smith found?

(11) What could Roman Catholics do in good conscience for the first time on 5 December 1966?

(12) Who was the author of the *Wealth of Nations* in 1776?

(13) Who completed his *Tractatus Logicophilosophicus* in a World War I Italian prisoner-of-war camp?

(14) Who was Peter Abelard's famous lover?

(15) What were this man's words when he stepped into history on 21 July 1969?
▽

16   Which oriental sage's philosophical observations are
     recorded in the *Analects*?
     a) Confucius   b) Buddha   c) Muhammad

17   What does the Bible call the beginning of wisdom?

18   What religion did Adolf Hitler profess?

19   What's the sacred river of India?

20   Who is the French philosopher, who was led to the
     proposition 'I think, therefore I am'?

21   What country did Winston Churchill once describe as 'a
     riddle, wrapped in a mystery, inside an enigma?'

22   Which pope died thirty-three days after his election?

24   Which English Renaissance philosopher was the subject
     of Robert Bolt's play *A Man For All Seasons*?

25   Who is this well-known feminist writer and thinker?
     ▽

△
23   Which ancient Greek philosopher lived in a tub?

(1) Who rode a donkey named Dapple?

(2) Who is this hero of a play by Edmond Rostand?
▽

(3) Who was this character in love with?   ▷

(4) What is Madame Bovary's first name?

(5) Which empire's decline is described by Edward Gibbon?

(6) What was the sequel to *Little Women*?

(7) What was the chorus of the song sung by the blind pirate who came to call at the Admiral Benbow Inn?

(8) What was Emily Brontë's first and last novel?

(9) Where was John Bunyan when he wrote the first part of *The Pilgrim's Progress*?

(10) Who is Anna Karenina's aristocratic lover?

(11) Which 18th-century novelist wrote *Roderick Random*, *Peregrine Pickle* and *Humphrey Clinker*?

(12) What is the name of Mr George Knightley's home in Jane Austen's novel *Emma*?

(13) In which of Thomas Hardy's novels is Bathsheba Everdene the central figure?

(14) Who was the author of *Ivanhoe*?

16. Who invented this character?

17. Which English woman writer wrote *North and South*?

18. Which novel by Stephen Crane won him immediate recognition when it was first published in 1895?

19. Which novel by Émile Zola depicts life in a great mining community?

20. Which was D. H. Lawrence's first published novel?

21. Which of Voltaire's works is a famous satire on the optimism of Rousseau and Leibnitz?

15. What was the name of the girl on which this fictional character was based?

22. On which two rivers did Henry David Thoreau make an excursion in 1839, which he published in 1845 under the title *A Week on* . . . ?

23. Which great Russian novelist wrote *Fathers and Sons*

24. How many 'Barsetshire' novels did Anthony Trollope write?

25. In which of James Joyce's novels does Molly Bloom appear?

1. One of the moons of which planet was the destination in *2001: A Space Odyssey*?

2. What is this heavenly body?
▽

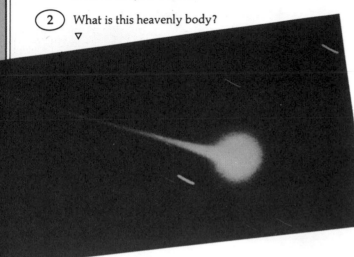

3. Which constellation is known as the Water Bearer?

4. What is the earth's galaxy called?

5. Which Polish astronomer demonstrated in 1512 that the sun is the centre of the solar system?
▽

6. Which planet has the shortest year?

7. What is the largest satellite orbiting Earth?

8. What is the longest possible duration of a solar eclipse?

9. What is the outermost part of the sun's atmosphere called?

10. Which planet is best known as both the morning and evening star?

11. Who was the Danish astronomer who wore a false nose made from gold, silver and wax?

12. Who had a hit with the song *Urban Spaceman*?

13. Which is the nearest star to Earth?

14. Which lies further from the sun?
a) Pluto b) Mercury c) Mars

15. Which ancient civilization worshipped this sun god?

16. What fraction of the Earth's gravity is the moon's?

17. How many stars make up Orion's belt?

18. Who played the lead in the movie *The Man Who Fell To Earth*?

19. Which of the planets was the subject of a flyby of *Voyager 1* in November 1980?

20. Which of the stars seen from Earth is also known as the Dog Star?

21. Which planet has two dwarf satellites called Phobos and Deimos?

22. What does a heliologist study?

23. Who is this Italian astronomer, who constructed the first astronomical telescope but had to give up his theories for religious reasons?
    ▷

24. In *Abbott and Costello Go To Mars,* which planet do Bud and Lou visit?

25. Which planet is this?
    ▽

1. What liquid does a chef coddle eggs in?

2. What agricultural cargo was HMS *Bounty* carrying when the famous mutiny broke out in 1789?

3. What is the principal ingredient of halva?

4. From the milk of which animal is Roquefort cheese made?

5. What cold soup was created in 1910 for the opening of New York City's old Ritz Carlton Hotel roof garden?

6. How many times were the original 'biscuits' baked?

7. Which explorer introduced pasta into the Italian diet?

8. Which Dickens character asked for more?
▽

9. How many times did William Ewart Gladstone reputedly chew each mouthful of food?
a) 12 b) 22 c) 32

10. Only one food produced by insects is widely eaten by man. What is it?

11. Who was the first to deep freeze food successfully?

12. Which contains the highest number of calories per ounce?
a) roast beef b) roast veal c) roast chicken

13. Where was this vegetable first cultivated?

▽

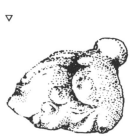

14. What is a 'tbsp' to a chef?

15. What does Bombay Duck consist of?

(16) To which fish family does the anchovy belong?

(17) Which spice is 'azafran' to a Spanish cook?

(18) What are grissini?

(19) Tied together, what do a sprig of parsley, thyme and a bay leaf comprise?

(20) What is the meaning of the cooking term 'farci'?

(21) Who was prompted by sights like this to comment: 'The French will only be united under the threat of danger. Nobody can easily bring together a country that has 265 kinds of cheese'?

▽

(22) From which animal does prosciutto come?

(23) Who kicked off her cookbook career with the publication of *The French Chef*?

(24) What did Shakespeare call '... the food of love' at the opening of *Twelfth Night*?

(25) Which famous breakfast food was first produced by Seventh Day Adventists in Battle Creek, Michigan?

1. Where is the Blue Grotto?

2. Which resort peninsula curves 65 miles (104 km) to its tip?

3. Which island group has Las Palmas as part of it?

4. Which country would you come up in if you drilled a hole straight through the Earth from Buenos Aires?

5. Which gate opens on East and West Berlin?
   ▽

6. What imaginary line encircling the earth is 90° from both poles at every point?

7. In which country is the Alhambra Palace?

8. Where in America is Great Salt Lake?

9. What is the traditional garment worn by Japanese women called?

10. Where do you pass through the Pedro Miguel Lock?

11. Which country do Walloons come from?

12. Of which city is this the symbol?
    ▽

13. Which is the only Arab country without a desert?

14. Which river flows past the Temple of Karnak?

15. What can you call yourself if you were born within the sound of London's Bow bells?

16. Where in the words of Noël Coward's song *Mad Dogs and Englishmen* do they 'strike a gong/And fire off a noonday gun'?

17. Where did this actor have the ultimate tango?
    ▷

(18) Which Scandanavian city is often called 'The Venice of the North'?

(19) At which British castle would you expect to see men dressed like this on guard? ▷

(20) In which region of the Soviet Union did the Chernobyl nuclear reactor accident occur?

(21) On the whole, where would W. C. Fields rather have been?

(22) Which Shah built this fine example of Mogul architecture?
▽

(25) Which nation's famine inspired this man to feed the world?
▽

(23) Which country's capital is Lagos?

(24) Which Caribbean island was invaded by American-led forces in October 1983?

1. How many shots did Harry fire in the opening bank-robbery scene of *Dirty Harry*?

2. Which punk rock group did Ronald Biggs sing with in Australia?

3. In which film did Rod Steiger play the part of Police Chief Bill Gillespie?

4. How many people were there in Bonnie and Clyde's gang?

5. What did Inspector Dreyfus use to cut the ends of his cigars in *A Shot in the Dark*?

6. Which drug bust yielded 81 pounds (36.7 kg) of heroin in 1962?

7. Which character in *Hill Street Blues* is known as 'Pizza Man'?

8. How are these stars of *Kojak* related off screen?

▽

9. Who played the gruff Dan Mathews in *Highway Patrol*?

10. Which film starred Al Pacino as a New York cop exposing police corruption?

11. What was the Pink Panther in the movie of the same name?

12. Which popular American TV crime series was spawned from the novel *Poor Poor Ophelia*?

13. Which TV series about New York cops which began in 1958 starred John McIntire and James Franciscus?

14. In which police series did this actress star from 1975 to 1978?

▽

(15) What is the name of the cop 'serenaded' in one of the numbers in *West Side Story*?

(16) Which 18th-century English highwayman did David Weston play for Walt Disney in 1965?

(17) Which force of 'movie' police did Ford Sterling lead?

(18) Who played the cop, out to get the gangsters who murdered his wife, in *The Big Heat*?

(19) Which British rock star played John McVicar in the movie that took his name? ▽

(20) What is Maigret's first name?

(21) Who is this pop star, who became a dandy highwayman in 1981? ▷

(22) Which half of Starsky and Hutch was actor Paul Michael Glaser?

(23) In which American city police force did Lee Marvin serve in the late fifties in M-Squad?

(24) Which detective fell to his death, but was successfully revived eight years later?

(25) Which 1930 film made this actor a star and featured the famous last line, '. . . is this the end of Rico'?
▽

(1) Who were 'overpaid, oversexed and over here'?

(2) Which famous World War II aircraft are flying here?
▽

(3) What began with the code signal, 'Climb Mount Niitaka'?

(4) Which country declared war on both the Allies and Germany in World War II?

(5) What is the infamous contraction of *Geheime Staatspolizei*?

(6) Who danced a jig at Compiègne, France in 1940?

(7) Which two countries fought the battle of the Coral Sea?

(8) What was the name given to Hitler's *blitzkrieg* offensive against the USSR in June 1941?

(9) Who was inspired to write, produce, co-direct and star in the 1942 movie *In Which We Serve* on hearing of the sinking of this man's destroyer?
▽

(10) Which city was the capital of Free China during World War II?

(11) Which country suffered the most combat deaths in World War II?

(12) Which country did the Allies invade in World War II's *Operation Avalanche*?

(13) Which part of Britain was occupied by the Germans in World War II?

14) Who said, after being bombed, 'Now I feel I can look the East End in the face'?

15) In which year during World War II did Winston Churchill become British prime minister for the first time?

16) Where were Omaha, Juno and Gold beaches?

17) What did Winston Churchill call this garment?

▽

18) Which World War II leader dallied with Clara Petacci?

19) Who was the American ambassador to the court of St James at the outbreak of World War II?

20) Who betrayed Norway to the Nazis?

21) Which of Hitler's deputies parachuted into Scotland to ▷ negotiate peace terms?

22) Which country did the battle of El Alamein take place in?

23) What is this mark?
▽

24) What was the codename for the Normandy invasion?

25) Where in September 1942 did Australian forces halt a Japanese land advance in the south-west Pacific?

(1) In which city did Shakespeare set the story of *Romeo and Juliet*?

(2) Who wrote the score for the 1948 musical based on *The Taming of the Shrew*?

(3) From which of Shakespeare's plays did this writer take the title for her long-running play *The Mousetrap*?

(4) Who is Jessica's father in *The Merchant of Venice*?

(5) According to tradition Shakespeare shares his birthday with which famous figure in English folklore?

(6) What is the 'sack' of which Sir John Falstaff is so fond in *Henry IV* ?

(7) How does Antigonus die in Act III scene 3 of *The Winter's Tale*?

(8) Who is Viola's brother in *Twelfth Night*?

(9) Which Japanese film director adapted *King Lear* to create *Ran*?

(10) Which of Shakespeare's heroines speaks the lines, 'O brave new world/That has such people in't'?

(11) This great English actor organized a jubilee in Shakespeare's memory at Stratford-on-Avon in 1769. Who is he?

(12) What other name is Robin Goodfellow given in *A Midsummer Night's Dream*?

(13) Who is this man, to whom Shakespeare dedicated *Venus and Adonis* in 1593?

(14) Who is Donalbain's father in *Macbeth*?

(15) Which military conflict forms the background for *Troilus and Cressida*?

(16) Who is told 'Beware the ides of March' by a soothsayer in one of Shakespeare's plays?

△

(22) On which play by Shakespeare was this musical based?

(23) Who agrees to marry Benedick at the end of *Much Ado About Nothing*?

(24) In which country do Antony and Cleopatra end their lives?

(25) In which forest does Shakespeare set part of *As You Like It*?

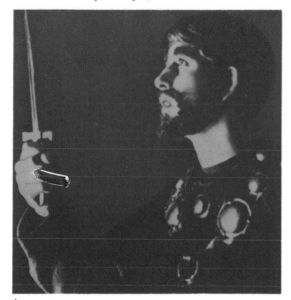

△

(17) This performer's Macbeth was outstanding by schoolboy standards, according to one critic. Who is the budding thespian?

(18) Who opens the play that bears his name with the lines:
   Now is the winter of our discontent
   Made glorious summer by this sun of York; ?

(19) In which of his plays did Shakespeare write one scene entirely in French?

(20) What was the Christian name of the son that Anne Hathaway bore Shakespeare?

(21) What specific individual item did Will Shakespeare leave Anne Hathaway in his will?

1. What was the cargo at the centre of the 1964 film *The Train*?

2. Which mountain can you see from the window of a train called the *Bullet*?

3. Who in the song drove the *Cannonball Express*?

4. In which European country is the famous Jungfraujoch railway station?

5. Which European country has a fast train known by the initials TGV?

6. In which continent is the world's longest stretch of straight railway track?

7. In which American state was the first North American transcontinental railway completed on 10 May 1869?

8. Which underground railway system links San Francisco with Oakland in California?

9. What significant 'first' did this musician achieve with his *Chattanooga Choo Choo* on 10 February 1942?

▽

△

10. This American writer once produced a comic story based on the noise of train wheels. Who is he?

11. Who was the artist who painted *Rain Steam and Speed, the Great Western Railway* in 1844?

12. Which city had the first subway dug?

13. Who in the film detonated the explosives which blew up the railway bridge over the River Kwai?

14. Which city is the western terminus of the Trans-Siberian railway?

15. Who composed this musical about trains? ▷ ▷ ▷ ▷ ▷

16. Where on an American freight train might you find a 'caboose'?

17. What unfortunate distinction does William Huskisson hold in railway history?

18. Into which British river did the railway bridge spanning it collapse in a gale while a train was crossing on 28 December 1879?

19. Where is the largest train station in the world?

20. What did the B & O railroad's initials stand for?

21. Which European city's subway system is called the Metropolitana?

22. What is a 'pandrol' in the world of railways?

23. What is the title of this film, set largely on a railway ▷ station?

24. What distinguishes the Khargpur Platform, West Bengal, India, from other railway platforms?

25. Who changed trains in Christopher Isherwood's novel of 1935?

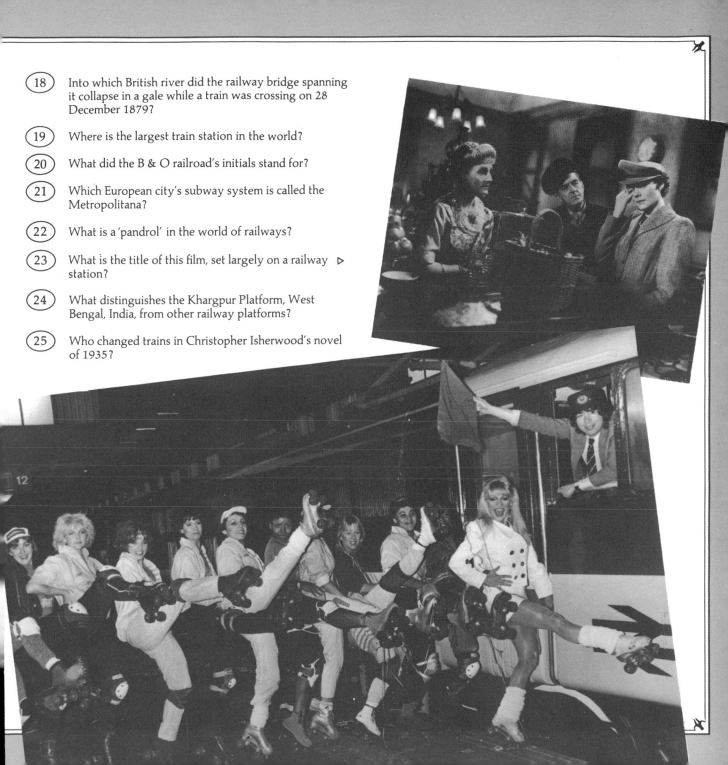

1. Who was the Czech gymnast who publicly opposed the 1968 Russian invasion of her country and later that year won four Olympic gold medals and two silvers?

2. Who defected at the 1975 American Tennis Open championship?

3. In which country was Maria Bueno born?

4. What was the first name of the donor of the Wightman Cup?

5. Who is this British rider who became the 1971 European three day event champion?
▽

8. This is the first-ever gymnast to score a maximum of 10.00 points in an Olympic gymnastics competition. Who is she?
▽

6. In which sport did Venezuela's Ana Maria Carrasco become world champion?

7. America's Valerie Brisco-Hooks won two Olympic track and field gold medals in the 1984 Olympics. One was for the 200 metres event – what was the other for?

9. Which swimmer won the 100 metres freestyle in the Olympic women's competition in 1956, 1960 and 1964?

10. Who rode *Be Fair*, *Wideawake*, *George* and *Killaire* to victory at the Badminton Horse Trials?

11. In which sport was Irina Rodnina a world champion?

12. Who was *Sports Illustrated*'s first female Sportsman of the Year?

13. Which former swimming champion starred in the films *Bathing Beauty* and *Take Me To The Ball Game*?

14. What was this woman the first to run in less than four and a half minutes? ▷

15. Which Russian gymnast was greeted by American President Richard Nixon in 1974 with the words: 'I have always been impressed by the way you land on your feet'?

16. In which year did women first compete in the Olympic Games?
a) 1908 b) 1928 c) 1900

17. Who won the 1976 women's singles at the French Open tennis championship?

18. In which sport did Switzerland's Christine Stückelberger win a gold medal in 1976?

19. Who was the first woman golfer to earn a million?

20. Which European athlete collected gold medals in the women's 100 metres, 200 metres, 80 metres hurdles and 4 × 100 metres relay at the 1948 Olympic Games?

21. In which year did Suzanne Lenglen win Olympic gold medals in the women's tennis singles and mixed doubles?

22. Which British woman tennis star was five times runner-up for the world table tennis championships?

23. In which sport is Maureen Flowers a force to be reckoned with by both men and women?

24. What woman champion first skated at the Olympics at the age of 11?

25. What swimming 'first' did America's Gertrude Ederle achieve in August 1926?

(1) On which island would you see statues like this?

(2) Which Tokyo street glitters with famed department stores and nightclubs?

(3) Which countries does the Mont Blanc Tunnel join?

(4) Which mountain does all of Cape Town look up to?

(5) Where is Dam Square?

(6) Where is the original Raffles Hotel?

(7) In which present-day country is the ancient city of Ephesus, once visited by St Paul?

(8) What palace is found on the site of James I's mulberry orchard?

(9) In which British city is the Royal Liver Building?

(10) Where would you step out to see the Giant's Causeway?

(11) Which mountain range is traversed by Kicking Horse Pass?

(12) Which capital city overlooks the Tagus River?

(13) What is the name given to this fountain?
▽

(14) In which Indian city is the Taj Mahal?

△

(15) Which of Paris's boulevards links the Arc de Triomphe with the Place de la Concorde?

△

(16) What is the street address of this house?

(17) Which canal spelled backwards is a Greek god?

(18) What was once called Martin's Vineyard?

(19) What Manhattan edifice has ten million bricks in it?

(20) What colour are the castellated walls of the Kremlin?

(21) Which civilization's legendary lost city can be seen at Machu Picchu?

(22) Which London landmark has an eleven foot (3.3 m) long hand?

(23) Which river does the longest railway bridge in the world span?

(24) Which Rome tourist attraction has one hundred and thirty-eight steps?

(25) What word did this famous sign originally spell out?

▽

1. Which comic-strip canine was born at the Daisy Hill Puppy Farm?

2. What is the name of this comic-strip character?

9. What are the names of Donald Duck's nephews?

3. What was the title of the first Peanuts gang TV special?

4. Who exclaimed 'Holy Barracuda!'?

5. What is comic-strip photographer Peter Parker's secret identity?

6. On which planet was this hero born? ▷

7. Which swamp-dwelling comic-strip character ran for American president in 1952?

8. How is Supergirl related to Superman?

(10) What is the famous surname of Popeye's friend J. Wellington?

(11) Which cartoon film proved to be the second biggest box office draw of 1969?

(12) **What is Snoopy called in Norway?**

(13) What was the name of the Flintstones' pet dinosaur?

(14) Which comic-strip character married horn-helmeted Helga?

(15) Who is this character's canine companion?

▽

(16) Which randy cat, of underground comic fame, was created by Robert Crumb?

(17) Which cartoon character is actually a *Geococcyx californianus*?

(18) Which comic-strip superheroine's secret identity is Diana Prince?

(19) What is the first thing Clark Kent removes during his transformation?

(20) Which cartoon character used Clarence Nash's voice to entertain us over the years?

△

(21) Which birthday did Popeye celebrate in 1979?

(22) Which Batman villain usually carried an umbrella?

(23) Which member of the Peanuts gang once said, 'There's no heavier burden than a great potential'?

(24) Who created the cartoon character Blondie?

(25) Which comic-strip superhero did C. C. Beck create?

(1) What sort of dinosaur is pictured here?
▽

(11) This shy relative of the giraffe has remained almost unchanged for 30 million years. What is it?
▽

(2) What is the largest animal ever known to have lived?

(3) Who published *The Origin of Species* in 1859?

(4) Which modern animal is descended from the Eohippus?

(5) How did the earliest settlers arrive in North America?

(6) In which country were the remains of Neanderthal man discovered?

(7) What is palaeontology?

(8) What was the first construction material manufactured by man?

(9) Which period was earlier in geological time — the Triassic or the Cretaceous?

(10) In which film did this actress grunt her way to   ▷
international stardom?

12. On which continent did early man first develop, according to most scientists?

13. What has made the Lascaux cave in south-west France famous?

14. In which African country is Lake Turkana, famous for its remains of early man?

15. What animal is being hunted here?
▽

16. What 'age' in man's development immediately followed the Bronze Age?

17. Which 'prehistoric' skull was found to be a forgery in 1955?

18. What is the more common name for our early ancestor *Sinanthropus pekinensis*?

19. Who was Fred Flintstone's neighbour with whom he was always getting into trouble?

20. After which prehistoric animal was this man's pop group named?.
▷

21. In which film, shot at Lyme Regis in Dorset, did Jeremy Irons play a Victorian fossil hunter?

22. What was Pangaea?

23. Which animal, that has remained virtually unchanged since prehistoric times, is the only mammal flying today?

24. Which film company released *One of Our Dinosaurs is Missing* in 1975?

25. Where in the Southern Hemisphere would you find that prehistoric survivor the lizard-like Tuatara?

1. Which English word comes from the old French *covrefeu*, meaning 'cover fire'?

2. Which letter begins the fewest words in the English language?

3. What does 'U' stand for in I.O.U.?

4. What is this animal and what do you call more than one of them?
▽

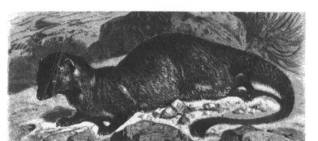

5. What do 'Mc' and 'Mac' mean when used in surnames?

6. What does a bibliophile enjoy?

7. Which is the most commonly used punctuation mark?

8. Which is the second most common word in written English?

9. Which letter accounts for one of every eight used in written English?

10. What is the name of the man who has been immortalized in a word that describes his prudish editing of the works of Shakespeare?

11. There is only one genuine English word that ends in the letters 'amt'. What is it?

12. Which letter in the English alphabet once went by the name of 'izzard'?

13. Which six-letter English word can mean 'to stick fast' as well as meaning the complete opposite?

14. Which seven-letter English word uses no vowels?

15. What is the plural of 'opus'?

16. Which word occurs more frequently in the Bible: Jehovah or Lord?

17. Which common three-letter word was coined by the Dutch scientist J. B. van Helmont from the Greek word *chaos*?

18. What did H. L. Mencken call: 'The most shining and successful Americanism ever invented'?

19. Was the word 'news' first used with a singular or plural meaning?

(20) Whose political aspirations accompanied the 1968 slogan 'Let's Get America Going Again'?

(21) What does the acronym AWOL stand for?

(22) Which grammatical term is given to words that sound like the thing they describe?

(23) In which of Sheridan's plays does the original perpetrator of the malapropism appear?

(24) What is the opposite of nadir?

(25) What is the name given to slips of the tongue such as, 'You hissed my mystery lecture', which this man was famous for making?

▽

.g., *n*. Construction of electrical engine equipment. **electronic engineering**, *n*. Co struction of electronic equipment and apparatu **hydraulic engineering**, *n*. The construction waterworks, the application of water-power, t construction of dams, docks, etc. **mechanic: engineering**, *n*. The construction of engines an machinery. **military engineering**, *n*. The cor struction of fortification, and of roads, bridges, etc used for military purposes.

*engird (en gĕrd'), *v.t.* (*past and p.p.* **engirt**) T encircle, to encompass, as with a girdle.
engirdle (en gĕr' del), *v.t.* To surround with or as with a girdle.

English (ing' glish) [A.-S. *Englisc*, *Ænglisc*, from *Engle*, the Angles], *a*. Pertaining to England or its inhabitants; spoken or written in the English language; characteristic of or becoming an English-man. *n*. The language of the British Isles, N. America, Australasia, parts of S. Africa, and other parts of the British Commonwealth; in printing, a size of type between great primer and pica; the people of England; the soldiers fighting on the English side. *v.t.* To translate into the English language; to express in plain English. **Basic English** [BASIC]. **Queen's, King's English**: Cor-rect English as spoken by educated people. **Middle English**: The English language in use from about 1150 to 1500. **Old English**: The English language in use before 1150, also called Anglo-Saxon; (*Print.*) [BLACK-LETTER]. **plain English**: Plain, unmistakable terms. **English bond**: (*Brick-laying*) Bonding by means of alternate courses of headers and stretchers. **Englishism**, *n*. **English-man, -woman**, *n*. A native or a naturalized inhabitant of England; one of English blood. **Englishness**, *n*. ***Englishry**, *n*. The quality or state of being an Englishman; *the part of the population of a country that is of English blood, esp. the English settlers in Ireland and their descendants; *the English population, the English quarter.

*englut (en glŭt') [O.F. *englotir*, L. *ingluttire* (IN-, *gluttire*, to swallow); and in later senses formed from EN-, GLUT], *v.t.* To swallow; to gulp down, to glut, to satiate.

engorge (en gŏrj') [F. *engorger* (EN-, *gorge*, GORGE)], *v.t.* To swallow up, to devour; (*in p.p.*) to fill to excess; (*Path.*) to congest (with blood). **engorge-ment**, *n*.

engraft (en graft'), *v.t.* To graft upon, to insert (a scion of one tree) upon or into another; to incor-porate; to implant, instil; to superadd.

engrail (en grāl') [O.F. *engresler*, perh. from *gresle* (F. *grêle*), hail], *v.t.* (*chiefly in Her.*) To indent in curved lines, to make ragged at the edges as if broken with hail; (*poet.*) to adorn. **engrailment**, *n*.

engrain (en grān'), *v.t.* *To dye in fast colour. dye deeply; (*fig.*) to impl...

(1) What is the meaning of this mathematical symbol?

∴

(2) What is this musical symbol called?

, ,

(3) Which gas is represented by the chemical formula CO?

(4) Which sign of the zodiac is represented by this symbol?

MARCH

(5) With which participants in World War II was this symbol associated?

(6) To which of the planets does this refer?

♄

(7) What does this Greek letter represent in geometry?

Π

(8) Which metal is given the symbol Au?

(9) Which of the sun's planets is represented by this symbol?

⊕

(10) What does this signify in mathematics?

≠

(11) Which sign of the zodiac is represented by this symbol?

APRIL

(12) What connection does the chemical represented by the letters Ne have with electric lighting?

(13) What does this symbolize in biology?

(14) Which Nobel-prize-winning husband and wife discovered the element Ra?

(15) What does this signify in mathematics?

(16) Which chemical element is represented by the letters Ca?

(17) What is the meaning of this astronomical symbol?

(18) What does this mean in mathematics?

(19) What is the meaning of this in the commercial world?

(20) What does this symbolize in biology?

(21) Which heavenly body is represented by this symbol?

(22) Which sign of the zodiac is represented by this symbol?

JANUARY

(23) What is the chemical symbol for magnesium?

(24) What does this symbol signify?

(25) This is the symbol of which sign of the zodiac?

SEPTEMBER

1　Which game features the largest ball?

2　Who was awarded a four-pound (1.8 kg) gold soccer ball after scoring his 1000th goal?

3　Which ball game is played with this?

4　Which of snooker's so-called coloured balls has the lowest points value?

5　Which famous cricket trophy is David Gower holding in this picture?

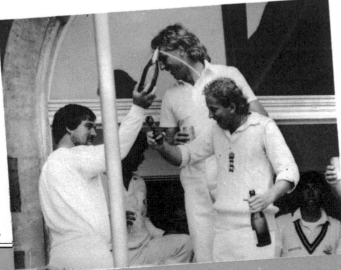

6　Which New York City residential area is home to the West Side Tennis Club?

7　How many players are there on each side in this game?

8　What sport's racket allows no more than fifty pimples per square centimetre?

9　Which country dominated Olympic hockey from 1928 until 1960?

10　Which is bigger – a polo ball or a softball?

11　Which American civilization played a ball game called *ollamalitzli* in which players propelled a solid rubber ball through a fixed stone ring?

12　What sported pimples before switching to dimples?

13　What did Joe Sobek originally call his 1950 invention that is today known as racquetball?

14　Which side of a tennis receiver's court is the deuce court?

(15) Which ball game did George Hancock invent in Chicago in 1887?

(16) What colour is the 3-ball in pool?

(17) In which ball game did Geoffrey B. Hunt of Australia rise to become World Champion?

(18) Which sport's ball has thirty-two panels?

(19) How many times is a volleyball team allowed to contact the ball before returning it to the other court?

(20) What are you trying to do at break point in tennis?

(21) Which coloured ball partners blue in a game of croquet?
a) black   b) red   c) yellow

(22) Which widespread racket game *doesn't* use a ball?

(23) Who is this famous sportsman?

(24) Which has the smaller number of players on each side – Rugby Union or Rugby League?

(25) Which country's national sport is this?

1. The Kalahari Desert lies mainly within the borders of which African country?

2. What is the name given to the area of the Arabian peninsula crossed by Wilfred Thesiger's party in 1946?

3. Which is larger – the Nubian Desert or Australia's Great Sandy Desert?

4. Of which country is this the capital?
▽

5. In what year did Roald Amundsen's party first reach the South Pole?
a) 1901   b) 1907   c) 1911

6. What type of camel would you expect to find in the desert regions of central Asia?

7. With the deserts of which continent are the names of Ludwig Leichardt, Charles Sturt and Robert O'Hara Burke associated?

8. On which side of the Andes does the Atacama Desert lie?

9. After which American president was the ship named in which Robert E. Peary set sail to become the first man to reach the North Pole in 1909?
▷

10. Which two countries lie on either side of the Thar Desert?

11. What type of animal with enormous curving horns did Marco Polo sight high on the Pamir plateau and which now bears his name?
▽

(12) Which is the world's longest mountain range?

(13) What nationality was the first European to sight the Grand Canyon?

(14) Which two countries share what was originally called Patagonia?

(15) What is the title of Robert Flaherty's documentary film about life in the Arctic, released in 1921?
▽

(23) What is the title of this 1969 movie, filmed among some of America's most spectacular desert scenery?

(24) Which railway line, running from Damascus to Medina, was the target for T. E. Lawrence's raiding Arabs in World War I?

(25) Which town was the capital of the old territory of central Australia from 1926 to 1931?

(16) To which tribe do these people, known as 'the people of the veil', belong?   ▷

(17) About how many weeks did Jesus Christ spend in the wilderness?

(18) What size is Antarctica in relation to Africa?
a) $\frac{1}{2}$ b) $\frac{1}{3}$ c) $\frac{2}{3}$

(19) Who starred in the title role of the 1939 film *Beau Geste*?

(20) On which continent is the world's longest glacier?

(21) Which is larger – Canada's Great Bear Lake or its Lake Ontario?

(22) The Hoggar mountains lie at the centre of which of the world's great deserts?

1. Which song contains the lines, 'Someday when we're dreaming, Deep in love, Not a lot to say'?

2. In which American state would you expect to find corn 'as high as an elephant's eye'?

3. Which Elton John song goes, 'How wonderful life is, while you're in the world'?

4. What followed, 'It was an itsy-bitsy, teeny-weeny ...'?

5. Which Bob Dylan song begins, 'I ain't lookin' to compete with you, beat or cheat or mistreat you'?

6. What fruit, ... is impossible to eat,' according to a Trini Lopez song?

7. Which song begins, 'When the moon is in the seventh house'?

8. Which girl were this duo singing about with the line, 'You're shaking my confidence daily'?
▽

9. Why did Don MacLean refer to 3 February 1959 as, 'The day the music died'?

10. In which two songs did The Beatles sing, 'She loves you yeah, yeah, yeah'?

11. Which song contained the line, 'Be sure to wear some flowers in your hair'?

12. What kind of island did this man sing about?
▽

13. Where did Ralph McTell offer to 'take you by the han And lead you ...'?

14. Which of Marilyn Monroe's husbands gets a mention the song Mrs Robinson?

15. Who did the Beach Boys see when they went looking for romance?

16. To whom did Yul Brynner address the question, 'Shal we dance?' in the film of the musical The King and I?

17. Who sang, 'Every step you take, Every move you ma ... I'll be watching you'?

(18) Who did this man sing *High Hopes* for in the 1960 Presidential campaign?

▽

(19) What shouldn't you step on even if you, 'Burn my house, steal my car, drink my liquor from an old fruit jar'?

(20) What, according to Doris Day's 1956 hit, did her mother reply to the question, 'What will I be?'?

(21) What was the Manfred Man girl singing as she was 'Just walkin' down the street'?

(22) To which inventor of a famous medicinal compound did ▷ this band drink in 1968?

(23) Whose hideaway was, 'A dark and secluded place' in Johnnie Ray's 1955 song?

(24) Which Who song went, 'I was born with a plastic spoon in my mouth'?

(25) This singer had a hit with a song that included the line, 'Don't let them say your hair's too long, I don't care, with you I can't go wrong'. What was the name of her partner?

▷

1. Who was the British poet who joined Greek insurgents in their rebellion against the Turks in 1823, the year before his death?

2. What was this woman the first to do in 1932?
▽

△

9. Who is this British heroine?

10. Which civil rights hero has an epitaph which reads, 'Fre at last, free at last, thank God Almighty, I'm free at las

11. In which country was the famous British commander Charles George Gordon serving in 1863–4, when his military prowess placed him among the leading soldie of his day?

3. Which American suffragist is most famous for her fight for the right of women to wear trousers?

4. Which country numbers William Tell among its national heroes?

5. Which contemporary hero's autobiography is entitled *Is That It?*

6. What is the trade of this Polish hero?   ▷

7. In which of Shakespeare's plays does a character named Hero agree to marry another named Claudio?

8. What is the name of the only woman Pharoah?

△

(12) Which soldier is buried beneath this arch?

(13) Who directed Israel's campaigns in the 1967 and 1973 wars?

(14) Which Scottish hero travelled under the name Betty Burke?

(15) Which Nobel-prizewinning heroine of science was killed by her own discovery?

(16) Which nursing heroine was shot by the Germans in 1915 for her part in assisting British and Allied fugitives?

(17) Who, in an act of bravery, walked out of Scott's tent?

(18) Which island's entire population was awarded the George Cross?

(19) To which movement did the heroes and heroines of World War II's Maquis belong?

(20) Which naval hero said, 'England expects every man will do his duty'?

(21) Which heroine from the Middle Ages was born in the village of Domrémy?

(22) Which hero galloped from Boston towards Lexington on an April night in 1755 to warn that the British were coming?

(23) Which country's heroes are celebrated in Luis de Camoens's epic national poem *The Lusiads*?

△

(24) Which 17th-century North American heroine was daughter of Powatan and went to England in the last year of Shakespeare's life?

(25) Who helped her father rescue shipwreck survivors off the Farne Islands on 7 September 1838?

▽

1. What were the 'dolls' of Jacqueline Susann's *Valley of the Dolls*?

2. What 1956 Grace Metalious novel was on the best-seller list for two years?

3. What was the only book Margaret Mitchell wrote?

4. Which wife of one of the Beatles wrote the book *Grapefruit*?

5. What is this prolific author's favourite colour?
▽

6. What was 'Superwoman's' first fiction blockbuster?

7. What is the nationality of authoress Dame Ngaio Marsh?

8. Which writer disappeared after *The Murder of Roger Ackroyd*?

9. Who wrote the book on which this Steven Speilberg film is based?
▽

10. Whose biography is titled *Lady Sings the Blues*?

11. Which book of brothel reminiscences did Polly Adler write?

12. Who wrote *The Female Eunuch*?

13. Whose autobiography is entitled, *I Know Why the Caged Bird Sings*?

14. Who wrote the poem *Not Waving But Drowning*?

15. What name did crime writer Lady Mallowan write under?

16. Whose World War II diary ended with the author wondering what she'd be like, 'If there weren't any other people in the world'?

17. Whose novel, *The Country Girls*, was banned in Ireland for being, 'a smear on Irish womanhood'?

(18) Who is this famous movie star, doing anything but following the title of her autobiography, *Dancing in the Light*?

▽

(19) What was the first name of this author of the classic *Book of Household Management*?

▽

▷

(20) Her novel *Three Weeks* is said to have sold five million copies and her face became familiar among Hollywood screenwriters from 1920 to 1927 – who was she?

(21) Which young author had her first and last success with *The Young Visitors*?

(22) Who was made famous in 1920 by the publication of *Bliss and Other Stories*?

(23) Which novelist was born in Persia, lived in Southern Rhodesia from 1925 until 1949 and then commenced a series of novels set in Africa?

(24) What was the name of the author on whose life this film was based? ▽

(25) Who wrote the play *The Knack*?

(1) What did Count Alessandro Volta demonstrate to this French leader in 1801?

▽

(7) Who invented this, which went like a rocket in 1829?

▽

(2) Which fastener did Whitcomb Judson patent in 1893?

(3) What nationality was the inventor of the first printing press?

(4) What was Linus Yale's occupation?

(5) What is the name of the scientist who developed a means of destroying pathogenic micro-organisms by heat in 1867?

▷

(6) Where was Marconi's first transatlantic radio signal received on 12 December 1901?

8. Which tool did Charles Moncke invent?

9. What invention of Colonel Jacob Schick could be said to have changed the face of man when it appeared in 1931?

10. Who filed the first patent in America for a motion picture camera?

11. When was the disc brake first used on an aircraft?
a) 1933 b) 1943 c) 1953

12. This man invented the bifocal lens in 1780. Who is he?
▽

13. Which scientific instrument did Zacharias Janssen invent in 1590?

14. What did Gail Borden give to the world in 1853?

15. What was the subject of Konrad Röntgen's first X-ray photograph in 1895?

16. Who invented the railroad sleeping car in 1859?

17. What did Richard Gatling invent in 1861?

18. Who transmitted the first telephone message: 'Watson, come here, I want you'?

19. Which synthetic food was named by its inventor after the Greek word for a pearl?

20. What was Archimedes doing when he discovered the principle of buoyancy and exclaimed 'Eureka!'?

△
21. This 'analytical engine', invented by Charles Babbage, is the forerunner of what piece of modern technology?

22. What did Clarence Birdseye perfect in 1924?

23. Which synthetic material was invented at the Du Pont Labs, Seaford, Delaware in 1937 by Dr Wallace H. Carothers?

24. Which wheel did Blaise Pascal invent in a search for perpetual motion?

25. Who patented his waterproof coat in 1823?

1. Which skier won America's first ever Alpine skiing title at the Olympic Games?

2. Of which winter sport did Sir Arthur Conan Doyle become an early British exponent?

3. Which Swiss winter sports resort is the home of the Cresta Run?

4. What nationality is the slalom champion Ingemar Stenmark?

5. Where is the world championship sled dog race held each February?

6. Which 1965 Beatles' film featured this sequence?
▽

7. What has happened to a 'burned rock' in curling?

8. What is this?
▽

9. Which ski run has the bigger vertical drop – men's slalom or women's giant slalom?

10. What nationality was the competitor who commented: 'We may not be the greatest at winning Winter Olympics but at least we can carry our bloody flag properly'?

11. What fits into a snowshoe's bridle?

12. In which Austrian resort is the famous Hahnenkamm race held?

13. Which American city has hosted two Winter Olympics?

14. Which of the world's great mountains did Yuichiro Miura ski down on 6 May 1970?

15. Across which North American mountains did Snowshoe Thompson carry the mail on skis from 1856 to 1876?

△

△

16. Who is this winter-sport-loving royal?

17. In which Alpine resort did France's Jean-Claude Killy win three Olympic gold medals in 1968?

18. Which city hosted the first winter Olympics in Asia?

19. Why might Dante have approved of the world's longest downhill ski race held at Mürren in Switzerland?

20. Who wrote the music to which this pair danced to win their 1984 Olympic gold?

21. How far did Finland's Matti Nykanen jump at Planica, Yugoslavia when he made the longest ski-jump ever recorded on 17 March 1985 ?
a) 500 ft (152.4 m)   b) 610 ft (186 m)   c) 830 ft (253 m)

22. Which is faster, the highest speed achieved on skis or the highest on a toboggan?

23. From which language did English adopt the word *ski*?

24. Who wrote the book *Paa Ski Over Grönland*, published in 1890?

25. For which James Bond movie was a parachute ski-jump filmed from the summit of Canada's Mount Asgard?

Photographic Acknowledgments

Special thanks for major contributions to:
Walt Disney Productions, The Kobal Collection,
The Mansell Collection, National Portrait Gallery,
Syndication International, Steve Brown of Sporting
Pictures and the Topham Picture Library.

Other photographs are from:

Australian Tourist Authority, Ian Bradshaw, Camera
Press, Dee Conway, the Corcoran Collection,
E. T. Archive, John Frost Newspaper Service,
Hodder and Stoughton, Hulton Picture Library,
Johnstone Factfinders Inc., Monarchives,
Octopus Books, Phil Sheldon, David Street
Spectrum Colour Library, Zefa (UK) Ltd

The publishers have made every effort to correctly
identify photographs, but will be pleased to correct
errors or omissions in future editions.

PICTURE RESEARCH BY MARY CORCORAN

Additional research by Craig Dodd and Michael Johnstone

1 · G · Europe

1 The Volga
2 Paris – it is the top of the Eiffel Tower
3 Monaco – it is $3\frac{1}{2}$ miles (5.6 km) long
4 Belgrade
5 Luxembourg
6 Switzerland
7 Brindisi
8 Spain
9 Rotterdam
10 Czechoslovakia
11 The English Channel
12 The Shannon
13 Eros's
14 Hungary
15 Great Britain
16 Yugoslavia
17 Sweden
18 Denmark
19 a) Helsinki
20 Italy
21 In France – near Beauvais. The airship was the R101
22 France
23 Moscow
24 The Atlantic Ocean
25 Romania, which contains Transylvania – he is Count Dracula

2 · E · Mozart & Co

1 William Tell
2 Benjamin Britten (1913–76)
3 Wolfgang Amadeus Mozart (1756–91)
4 Madame Butterfly
5 *A Whiter Shade of Pale*
6 Roger Daltrey, in *Lisztomania* – the composer is Franz Liszt (1811–86)
7 One
8 'From the New World'
9 *The Magic Flute*
10 *The Dream of Gerontius*
11 The treble clef
12 The words
13 He composed the piano suite *Pictures from an Exhibition* in that year
14 Russian
15 The cello
16 *La Traviata*
17 Herbert von Karajan
18 The 'Unfinished' – the composer is Franz Schubert (1797–1828)
19 George I (1660–1727)
20 Thomas Tallis (c. 1505–85) – *Fantasia on a Theme of Tallis*
21 Crotchets
22 It is silent
23 Manuel de Falla (1876–1946)
24 Peter Ilich Tchaikovsky (1840–93)
25 Georg Philipp Telemann (1681–1767) – the instrument is the French horn

3 · H · Twentieth Century

1 Hilda – she is Margaret Thatcher
2 Abyssinia (today called Ethiopia) – he is Benito Mussolini (1883–1945)
3 Richard Nixon's
4 Romanov
5 The Treaty of Versailles
6 The Berlin Wall
7 48 stars
8 The Red Brigade
9 Konrad Adenauer (1876–1967)
10 Shah Mohammad Reza Pahlavi – the Shah of Iran
11 The *Lusitania* – torpedoed on 7 May 1915
12 In Munich
13 Four times
14 Vichy
15 Constantine II
16 Bolivia – he is Che Guevara (1928–67)
17 Albania
18 President Juan Peron died and was succeeded by his wife
19 He became Pope John Paul II
20 That of T. E. Lawrence (Lawrence of Arabia) (1888–1935)
21 In Sarajevo, Yugoslavia – they were Archduke Franz Ferdinand of Austria and his wife
22 The Red Baron – he was Baron Manfred von Richthofen (1882–1918)
23 The SS *Titanic* hit an iceberg and sank
24 In 1983
25 Gabrielle 'Coco' Chanel – the first woman to voluntarily get a suntan

4 · AL · Spies and Sleuths

1 John Le Carré
2 Perry Mason loses
3 Raymond Chandler (1888–1959)
4 James Bond
5 The Saint – Simon Templar
6 Graham Greene
7 A Ronson lighter
8 Ellery Queen
9 James Bond's
10 Bruce Wayne
11 Mickey Spillane
12 The CIA
13 Charlie Chan
14 Sherlock Holmes
15 Belgian
16 Ian Fleming
17 Pinkerton's
18 James Coburn
19 Lord Peter Wimsey
20 Erskine Childers (1870–1922)
21 Wilkie Collins (1824–89)
22 Mycroft
23 George Smiley
24 *The Maltese Falcon*
25 His secretary – Della Street

5 · SN · Birds

1 Scales
2 The albatross
3 The ostrich
4 Two
5 Alfred Hitchcock directed a movie called *The Birds* in 1963
6 The penguin
7 New Zealand – the bird is the kiwi
8 John James Audubon (1785–1851)
9 A swan
10 Richard Burton
11 One swallow
12 The chicken
13 An Arctic tern
14 The kiwi
15 *One Flew Over the Cuckoo's Nest* (1975)
16 Donald Duck
17 *Hotel California*
18 A jackdaw
19 Western Australia
20 The Little Sparrow – she is Edith Piaf (1915–63)
21 A skein
22 Paul Gallico (1897–1976)
23 America
24 Male bee hummingbird
25 Four and twenty

6 · SL · Soccer

1 Yankee Stadium – he is Pele
2 Argentina
3 FIFA – Fédération Internationale de Football Association
4 Bryan Robson scored against France after 27 seconds of play in 1982
5 Norwich City
6 Diego Maradona
7 Italy
8 AC Milan
9 Zico
10 Geoff Hurst in the 1966 final
11 Hungary
12 Jules Rimet
13 1930
14 Real Madrid
15 Fiji
16 Real Madrid
17 Kenny Dalglish
18 1984
19 Rio de Janeiro with its Maracana Stadium
20 Europe's leading goal scorer
21 Arsenal
22 Celtic
23 Italy
24 Liverpool
25 France

7 · G · World Titles

1 Sex Pistols
2 Perry Como
3 *The Philadelphia Story*
4 *An American in Paris*
5 Massachusetts – in the song of the same name
6 Mexico
7 *New York, New York* – made 1977 and starring Liza Minelli and Robert de Niro
8 Abba
9 In Dallas – they are the stars of the TV soap opera *Dallas*
10 Argentina
11 To Hollywood – they are British band Frankie Goes To Hollywood
12 Audrey Hepburn
13 *Algiers* (1938)
14 Arnhem – Netherlands
15 Singapore
16 *The Canterbury Tales*
17 At Peking – in *55 Days at Peking* (1963)
18 *From Russia With Love* (1963)
19 Harper Valley
20 London – the film is called *An American Werewolf in London*
21 In Marienbad
22 Manhattan
23 St Louis
24 Wisconsin
25 Dooley Wilson – as Sam

8 · E · The Hollywood Greats

1 Breakfast
2 Douglas Fairbanks Jr
3 Natalie Wood (1938–81)
4 Jayne Mansfield (1932–67)
5 Yul Brynner (1915–86)
6 Elizabeth Taylor's breasts
7 Parker
8 Omar Sharif
9 Charlie Chaplin (1889–1977) – the film was made in 1926 but not released because Chaplin threatened legal action
10 Clark Gable (1901–60)
11 'That was a great game of golf, fellers' – the star was Bing Crosby (1901–77)
12 Michael Caine
13 Jackie Coogan (1914–84) – child star who had his own production company
14 *True Grit*
15 *The Time Machine*
16 *The Graduate*
17 *The Colbys* – she is Barbara Stanwyck
18 Katharine Hepburn – she won the award for *The Lion in Winter* and Streisand for her performance in *Funny Girl*
19 Fred Astaire's
20 Citizen Kane – the actor is Orson Welles
21 By drowning
22 Walt Disney
23 *Gone With The Wind*
24 *A Midsummer Night's Dream* – in which Oberon appears. The actress is Merle Oberon (1911–79)
25 *Straw Dogs*

9 · H · Wild, Wild Women

1 Rose Kennedy (née Fitzgerald)
2 Clementine Churchill
3 b) $1 250 000 – she is Betty Grable (1916–73)
4 Tokyo Rose
5 Mae West
6 'A woman scorned'
7 Samson
8 Bernadette Devlin
9 In Rouen, France – the picture shows Joan of Arc (1412–31), the French patriot and martyr
10 American women
11 Nancy Reagan
12 Spencer
13 The River Thames – she was a Red Indian princess who married an Englishman and died at Gravesend in 1617
14 The parsonage at Haworth, West Yorkshire, England – the sisters are the Brontës
15 Queen Elizabeth I
16 Lot's
17 Dorothy Parker (1893–1967)
18 Pankhurst – Emmeline (1858–1928)founded the Suffragette movement in 1905
19 Archduchess Marie Louise of Austria
20 Mrs Sirimavo Bandaranaike – who first became prime minister of Sri Lanka in 1960
21 Princess Elizabeth (now Queen Elizabeth II)
22 A jolly swagman
23 The Virgin Mary
24 Joseph Stalin (1879–1953)
25 Norma Jean Baker (1926–62)

10 · AL · Bookshelf

1 One thousand and one
2 Eight
3 Chinese
4 Georges Simenon – the detective is Maigret, the actor is Rupert Davies
5 Aramis
6 Jackie Collins – sister of *Dynasty* star Joan
7 Thomas Mann (1875–1955)
8 My Struggle
9 *Nausea*
10 Zorba The Greek
11 Edgar Allen Poe (1809–49)
12 Karamazov – from *The Brothers Karamazov* by Fyodor Dostoevsky
13 Fourteen
14 Franz Kafka (1883–1924)
15 Chilean
16 Alexandre Dumas (1824–95) – the book was *La Dame aux Camellias*, the film was *Camille*, starring Greta Garbo
17 China
18 *One Day in the Life of Ivan Denisovitch*
19 Stephen Leacock (1869–1944)
20 An author
21 The University of Chicago – the book is the *Encyclopaedia Britannica*
22 It attracted the highest price paid for any book or work of art when sold at auction for £8 140 000

23 Marcel Proust (1871–1922)
24 Lemuel – in *Gulliver's Travels* by Jonathan Swift (1667–1745)
25 Patrick White

11 · SN · Machines

1 Thomas Alva Edison (1847–1931)
2 The windscreen wiper
3 An early clock – made of iron in the fourteenth century
4 Light Amplification by Stimulated Emission of Radiation
5 Raising water
6 Isambard Kingdom Brunel (1806–59)
7 Benjamin Franklin (1706–90)
8 Decypher German codes
9 Sir Christopher Cockerell
10 The cinema – the brothers are Auguste (1862–1954) and Louis (1864–1948) Lumière
11 Boston – Massachusetts
12 The washing machine
13 Vacuum cleaners
14 The AC electric motor – in 1888
15 A radio
16 The jet engine
17 'Mary had a little lamb'
18 The polaroid camera
19 Rover – it had the registration number JET 1
20 Tremors of earthquakes
21 The electrocardiograph
22 It accelerates charged atomic particles
23 The Tardis
24 By means of flowing water
25 Leonardo da Vinci (1452–1519)

12 · SL · Horses and Courses

1 Polo
2 Eight
3 The stirrups
4 Ten
5 The left
6 Ascot
7 Three stallions – *Darley Arabian*, *Byerley Turk* and *Godolphin Barb*
8 Belmont Park – Long Island, New York
9 Longchamp – Paris
10 The Melbourne Cup
11 Newmarket – England
12 William Lee 'Bill' Shoemaker
13 Lester Piggott
14 Virginia Holgate
15 Three-day event, or horse trials
16 Aachen
17 *Shergar*
18 Dr Hackenbush
19 1912
20 Seven
21 Queen Anne (1665–1714)
22 The Grand National
23 The Oaks
24 The Kentucky Derby
25 Dressage

13 · G · Disasters

1 *Queen Elizabeth*
2 Lightning
3 The San Andreas Fault
4 Tenerife in the Canary Islands
5 San Francisco
6 It sank the *Lusitania* in 1915
7 It was lost at sea
8 Los Angeles
9 Steve McQueen
10 Indonesia – the photograph shows the eruption of 1976
11 The *Hindenburg* – which was destroyed in May 1937
12 Amritsar
13 a) 1912
14 Bucharest
15 The Space Shuttle
16 The Richter Scale
17 Tracy
18 India
19 Malfunction of a nuclear power station
20 Jonestown
21 Beirut, Lebanon – it happened when a lorry bomb detonated inside the Marine Barracks
22 The Fastnet Race
23 Salang Tunnel – in Afghanistan
24 Bees
25 Washington – it is Mount St Helens

14 · E · Also known As

1 Mortimer
2 Satchmo – he is Louis Armstrong (1900–71)
3 Twiggy
4 Scott Joplin
5 Archibald Leach – who later became Cary Grant
6 Moby Dick – the whale on whom Herman Melville's novel is based
7 Zorro – strip cartoon and film hero
8 Marie Antoinette (1755–93)
9 Julius – he is better known as Groucho Marx (1890–1977)
10 Sarah Bernhardt (1844–1923) – French actress
11 Billy the Kid (1859–81) legendary American bandit
12 Phineas Taylor Barnum (1810–91) – American showman famous for his flamboyant publicity
13 Lord Haw-Haw – William Joyce (1906–46) was a British traitor who broadcast Nazi propaganda
14 Sammy Davis Jr
15 Frances Gumm – who became famous as Judy Garland (1922–69)
16 Tina Turner
17 Sleeping Beauty
18 Michael Caine
19 Joan Crawford (1906–77)
20 Albert – he was crowned George VI (1895–1952)
21 Johnny Rotten – lead singer with the Sex Pistols
22 John Merrick (1863–90) – known as the Elephant Man
23 Lon Chaney (1906–73)
24 John Wayne (1907–79)
25 Ringo Starr – drummer with The Beatles

15 · H · International Affairs

1 Benito Mussolini (1883–1945)
2 The American Revolution (War of Independence) – it shows the Boston Tea Party (1773)
3 Alaska
4 Andrew Johnson (1808–75) – the picture shows Abraham Lincoln (1809–65)
5 The Politburo
6 The International Red Cross
7 Los Angeles – on 5 June 1968
8 The Japanese surrender in World War II
9 Seven
10 London
11 Georgi Malenkov
12 Two – Abraham Lincoln (1865) and William McKinley (1901). The picture shows Queen Victoria, (1819–1901)
13 Menachem Begin
14 The Cuban Missile Crisis
15 The Office of Strategic Services
16 Moscow
17 St Helena – in the Atlantic
18 The Nationalists
19 Georges Pompidou (1911–74) – it is the museum of contemporary art on the Rue Beaubourg
20 China
21 The United Nations
22 World War I
23 Kampuchea (Cambodia)
24 Raiza
25 Lenin's

16 · AL · Characters

1 Jekyll and Hyde
2 Mrs Hudson
3 The Salvation Army
4 The Invisible Man
5 Leonard Nimoy – who played Spock in *Star Trek*
6 Spanish
7 Two
8 Long John Silver's – in *Treasure Island* by Robert Louis Stevenson (1850–94)
9 Galahad
10 Dr Kildare
11 White – he was the eponymous star of Herman Melville's *Moby Dick*
12 Constance – in *Lady Chatterley's Lover* by D. H. Lawrence (1885–1930)
13 F. Scott Fitzgerald (1896–1940)
14 *Women in Love* – by D. H. Lawrence (1885–1930)
15 Dulcinea – in *Don Quixote* by Miguel de Cervantes (1547–1616)
16 Godot – who fails to appear in *Waiting For Godot* by Samuel Beckett
17 Gollum – in *Lord of the Rings* by J. R. Tolkien (1892–1973)
18 A flying school
19 Cinderella
20 Robinson Crusoe
21 Scarlett O'Hara – in *Gone With The Wind* by Margaret Mitchell (1900–49)
22 The Godfather
23 Jay – in *The Great Gatsby* by F. Scott Fitzgerald (1896–1940)
24 Adam Bede – the novel is by George Eliot (1819–80)
25 Adam's

17 · SN · Time

1. Six months – with wet and dry seasons of equal length
2. The Mayas
3. Julius Caesar (c. 100–44 BC)
4. Salvador Dali
5. King Alfred
6. The chronometer
7. Caesium
8. They were shorter – about 21 hours long
9. 180°
10. Tide
11. One
12. c) 14 September
13. 15th century – by Bartholomew Manfredi in 1462
14. May or June – the sign is Gemini, which is generally accepted to cover the period 21 May to 21 June
15. 24
16. 16
17. Gregory Peck
18. 1 minute 40 seconds – or 100 seconds
19. Big Ben – it is officially called the Westminster clock, and is found at the Palace of Westminster, London
20. Ten
21. An astrolabe
22. Seven – New York is five hours behind London, seven hours behind Athens, one hour behind Bermuda and one hour in front of Mexico City
23. A means of dating archeological finds
24. Copenhagen – the clock is the Olsen Clock in the city's Town Hall
25. Salisbury Cathedral's faceless clock dates from 1386, or even earlier

18 · SL · Time Out

1. The Atlantic – it's one of the beaches of Rio de Janeiro
2. Istanbul – it is the Church of St Sofia
3. Switzerland
4. Belgium
5. Moscow
6. Alberta
7. Brazil
8. Barbados
9. Spain – it is Antonio Gaudi's *Sagrada Familia* in Barcelona
10. Yellowstone National Park – the geyser is Old Faithful
11. Cliff Richard
12. IATA – International Air Transport Association
13. Florida – EPCOT stands for Experimental Community of Tomorrow
14. Provence
15. The Vosges mountains – in eastern France
16. The Maldive Islands
17. Safari
18. The Seychelles
19. Portuguese
20. Mardi Gras – in New Orleans
21. France's Côte d'Azur
22. Neil Simon
23. The Treetops Hotel – 100 miles (160km) north of Nairobi, capital of Kenya
24. San Giminiano
25. France – the island is Mont-St-Michel

19 · G · The Explorers

1. Little America – established at the South Pole in 1933
2. Spain's – the man is Christopher Columbus (1451–1506), the discovery America
3. Plymouth
4. Roald Amundsen and his party
5. St Christopher
6. Swiss
7. Henry Hudson (d. 1611)
8. Christopher Columbus (1451–1506)
9. Amerigo Vespucci (1451–1512) – Florentine explorer after whom America is named
10. Eric Newby – he wrote a book entitled *A Short Walk in the Hindu Kush* about his adventures
11. Vasco da Gama (c. 1460–1524)
12. Sir Ranulph Fiennes – from September 1979 until August 1982 during which time it circumnavigated the globe through both poles
13. Sir Walter Raleigh (1582–1618)
14. St Brendan
15. Kublai Khan (1214–94)
16. Cheng Ho
17. Jacques Cartier (1491–1557)
18. Sir Richard Burton (1829–90)
19. HMS *Beagle*
20. The Sahara – crossing from Sierra Leone to Tangiers
21. The Niger – which he explored between 1795 and 1797
22. Falcon – he is Robert Falcon Scott (1868–1912)
23. The Northwest Passage
24. The second voyage (1772–73)
25. The Dutch

20 · E · Gossip Column

1. Jerry Lee Lewis – who was married to thirteen-year-old Myra Brown
2. Jerry Hall – who left pop star Bryan Ferry for Mick Jagger
3. Sammy Davis Jr
4. Roberto Rossellini – she is Ingrid Bergman (1915–82)
5. 1962 – on 5 August
6. Rachmanism – the man is Perec Rachman, who became infamous as a slum landlord
7. Frank Sinatra
8. Because she was discovered to be under age – she is Zsa Zsa Gabor seen with her mother and sisters
9. Eddie Fisher
10. *Jezebel*
11. Robert Wagner
12. Because he was divorced
13. Dr Kurt Waldheim
14. Maria Callas (1923–77)
15. Billie Jean King – American tennis star who admitted the affair
16. Koo Stark – ex-girlfriend of Prince Andrew
17. Liet. E. W. Spencer
18. The Steel Magnolia – she is Rosalynn Carter, wife of Jimmy Carter
19. Fleetwood Mac
20. Princess Grace of Monaco (1929–82) – killed in a car crash
21. Prince Aly Khan – the film star is Rita Hayworth
22. Groucho Marx (1890–1977)
23. Ian Botham
24. Spiro Agnew – American vice-president accused of tax-evasion and accepting bribes
25. Princess Michael of Kent – who discovered her father had been a Nazi

21 · H · Myths and Legends

1. Lady Godiva
2. Camelot
3. The gate of Hades
4. *Mad Max Beyond Thunderdome* – the leader is played by Tina Turner
5. Icarus
6. Noah
7. The Blarney Stone
8. William the Conqueror – he saw Halley's comet in April 1066
9. The left
10. Father Time
11. Remus
12. Astrology
13. Friday – named after Frigg or Freyja
14. Agamemnon
15. Atlas – who was condemned to hold up the sky for his part in the Titans' revolt against the gods
16. *Pygmalion* by George Bernard Shaw
17. Valhalla
18. The prophecies of the oracle – at Delphi
19. The Argonauts
20. T. H. White's *The Once and Future King* – the musical was *Camelot*
21. Sherwood Forest
22. Pegasus
23. Jacques Offenbach (1819–80)
24. Notre Dame – Paris
25. Gene Kelly – Xanadu is a mythical kingdom

22 · AL · Modern Masters

1. Piet Mondrian (1872–1944)
2. Pablo Picasso (1881–1973) – the style is Cubism
3. Sidney Nolan
4. Maurice
5. Gwen John (1876–1939) – sister of Augustus John (1878–1961)
6. Abstract art
7. Andy Warhol
8. *Wham!*
9. Mexican
10. Edgar Degas (1834–1917)
11. Queen Elizabeth II
12. Barbara Hepworth (1903–75)
13. Salvador Dali
14. Paul Gauguin (1853–1903)
15. Belgium
16. Henri Toulouse-Lautrec (1864–1901)
17. Claude Monet (1840–1926) and Edouard Manet (1823–83)
18. Vincent Van Gogh (1853–90)
19. Art Nouveau
20. David Hockney
21. Surrealism
22. Op (or Optical) Art
23. Jackson Pollock (1912–56)
24. Paul Klee (1879–1940)
25. Dadaism

23 · SN · Planet Earth

1. Summer
2. Amber
3. Greenpeace – the ship is the *Rainbow Warrior*
4. Water
5. Natural gas
6. Seven
7. The North Pole
8. The Arctic Circle
9. A stalactite
10. Pioneer 10 – the plaque carries details of the position of the Earth, its inhabitants, and Pioneer's course
11. The ebb tide
12. One ninth
13. South
14. Palaeontology
15. In summer
16. Purple
17. Permafrost
18. Diamonds
19. One per cent
20. AD 1
21. Major Tom – from the song *Space Oddity* by David Bowie
22. The North Pole
23. Marshall McLuhan (1911–82)
24. Dissolved salt
25. He is Gustav Holst (1874–1934) – the English composer of *The Planets*

24 · SL · Athletics

1. Wilma Rudolph
2. Shot put – he is Bruce Bennett, who starred as Tarzan
3. Triple jump
4. Harold Abrahams
5. Javelin
6. Seven events
7. 1968
8. Steve Cram
9. On your marks
10. Jesse Owens
11. Ron Clarke
12. Of the 1936 Berlin Olympics
13. Seven
14. Four – he is American athlete Carl Lewis
15. Bob Beamon – whose 29ft 2½in (8.90m) record still stands
16. Zola Budd
17. Greek – he was a shepherd named Spyridon Louis
18. Fifteen miles an hour
19. One lap to go
20. Three feet high
21. He ran it backwards
22. Seventeen years old
23. The foot race
24. Eric Liddell – the film is *Chariots of Fire*
25. Cuban

25 · G · World Records

1. New Guinea
2. Nigeria
3. Lake Ontario
4. The Amazon
5. Hudson Bay
6. China, with 13 frontiers
7. The Sahara
8. Mount Fuji in Japan
9. The USA-Mexico border
10. Reykjavik in Iceland
11. The Northern hemisphere
12. The USSR
13. The Gulf of Mexico
14. The Grand Canyon
15. The Vatican City
16. Canada
17. Second – it's also called K2
18. Damascus, capital of Syria – inhabited for c. 4500 years
19. c) Victoria Nyanza (Lake Victoria)
20. The Pacific Ocean
21. The Portuguese province of Macao – off the southern coast of China
22. The frontier between the USA and Canada
23. Jericho
24. Britain
25. The Caribbean

26 · E · Who Said . . .

1. a) Tallulah Bankhead (1902–68) – the other actresses are b) Lucille Ball and c) Gloria Swanson
2. *To Have and Have Not*
3. Tony Curtis
4. *The Kid*
5. *The Third Man* – although it was never actually spoken in the film
6. Dracula
7. Esther Williams
8. Jimmy Durante (1893–1980)
9. Louis B. Mayer (1885–1957)
10. Olly (Hardy) (1892–1957) said this to Stan (Laurel) (1890–1963)
11. Hedy Lamarr
12. Mr Chips – played in the 1939 movie *Goodbye Mr Chips* by Robert Donat
13. Orson Welles (1915–1986)
14. Fred Astaire and Ginger Rogers
15. 'Me no Leica'
16. c) Fred Astaire – the other stars are a) James Cagney and b) Danny Kaye
17. *The Maltese Falcon* – as Sam Spade
18. Julie Andrews
19. Alfred Hitchcock (1899–1980)
20. *A Day at the Races*
21. *Moby Dick*
22. *Some Like It Hot*
23. Mae West
24. Sam Goldwyn (1882–1974)
25. *Rebecca* – the line is addressed to Joan Fontaine

27 · H · Scandal

1. Michelle Triola
2. John Stonehouse – British politician and businessman
3. Marjorie Wallace – crowned Miss World in November 1973
4. He was serving a sentence for possessing marijuana
5. The Bunker Hunt brothers – Nelson and Herbert, who aspired to control the world supply of silver
6. Clifford Irving – the man pictured is Howard Hughes
7. Chamonix
8. Mary Jo Kopechne
9. Christine Keeler
10. Jean-Bedel Bokassa – former president of the Central African Republic
11. Prince Bernhard of the Netherlands
12. Lieutenant Earl Spencer
13. Joyce McKinney
14. Lord Lucan – known as Lucky
15. 'Big Bill' Tilden (1893–1953)
16. Alfred Dreyfus (c. 1859–1935)
17. William Randolph Hearst (1863–1951)
18. Christina Crawford – adopted daughter of actress Joan Crawford
19. George IV (1762–1830) – when he was Prince of Wales
20. Sid Vicious – of the Sex Pistols
21. The government of Portugal
22. Watergate – they are Carl Bernstein and Bob Woodward, the two *Washington Post* reporters who uncovered the story
23. Baccarat
24. In the United Kingdom – in 1720
25. The Pope – Pope John Paul I (1912–78)

28 · AL · Quote . . . Unquote

1. Oliver Cromwell (1599–1658)
2. 'East is east and west is west'
3. Rudyard Kipling (1865–1936) in *If*
4. Psalm 23
5. Surrender Dorothy
6. *Don Quixote* – by Miguel de Cervantes (1547–1616)
7. *On the Road*
8. James Thurber (1894–1961)
9. Adolf Hitler (1889–1945)
10. Aldous Huxley's *Brave New World* (1932)
11. The last word should be 'wife' not 'diversion'
12. Sherlock Holmes – created by Sir Arthur Conan Doyle and spoken in *The Red-Headed League*
13. *Peter Pan*
14. *A Tale of Two Cities*
15. Lillian Hellman (1907–84)
16. Benjamin Disraeli (1804–81)
17. b) Alfred J. Prufrock
18. A classic
19. Dorothy Parker (1893–1967)
20. James Joyce – the opening words of *Finnegan's Wake*
21. Eleventy-eleventh
22. Hubert Selby Jr's *Last Exit to Brooklyn*
23. 'The heart has its reasons' – from Pascal's *Pensées*, used as the title for the memoirs of the Duchess of Windsor (1896–1986)
24. Robert M. Pirsig's *Zen and the Art of Motorcycle Maintenance*
25. Lewis Carroll's *Alice*

29 · SN · The Human Body

1. Ten
2. The liver
3. The uterus – from the Greek word for 'womb' *hustera*
4. The middle finger
5. Four
6. One third
7. The lens
8. Blood – the four groups are A, B, AB and O
9. Smell
10. The eyes
11. 206 bones
12. Never
13. Intelligence Quotient
14. The common cold
15. The heel
16. At the tip
17. 23
18. Robert Pershing Wadlow (1918–40) – the tallest man ever measured, who stood 8ft 11.1ins (2.72m)
19. A finger-print
20. The eardrum
21. Vitamin C
22. 40
23. Enamel
24. The real name of the bone is the humerus – thus its nickname
25. Four – the picture shows a gathering of quadruplets. Madame Feodor Vassilyev gave birth to 69 children in 27 confinements, producing 16 pairs of twins, 7 sets of triplets and 4 sets of quadruplets

30 · SL · Sporting Greats – The Men

1. Weightlifting
2. O. J. Simpson
3. Franz Beckenbauer
4. Boxing gloves
5. Sir Donald Bradman
6. Floyd Patterson
7. Johann Cruyff – of the Netherlands
8. *The Greatest* – he is Muhammad Ali
9. Gene Tunney
10. Bruce Lee (1940–73)
11. Juan Manuel Fangio
12. Don Larsen
13. Albania
14. Arnold Palmer
15. Gloucestershire
16. Ty Cobb (1886–1961)
17. Aluminium
18. George Hermann (1895–1948)
19. All 49 of them
20. Rod Laver
21. Sir Stanley Matthews
22. Mark Spitz
23. Pele's
24. Jackie Stewart
25. Middleweight – the boxer is Marvin Hagler

31 · G · The Americas

1 French Guiana
2 The Galapagos Islands – the creatures are the giant tortoises which live there
3 George Vancouver (c. 1758–98)
4 Nazca
5 El Salvador
6 One – Ontario
7 USSR
8 Ecuador
9 Brasilia
10 Tin
11 Venezuela
12 Tierra del Fuego
13 The Colorado
14 Maine
15 Peru – the craft is Thor Heyerdahl's *Kon Tiki*
16 1620
17 Mexico City
18 The Mississippi
19 Argentina
20 Honolulu
21 Vermont
22 Chile and Ecuador
23 Lake Michigan
24 Venezuela's Angel Falls – at 3 212ft (979m) they're the highest on earth as well
25 Rockefeller Center

32 · E · The Silver Screen

1 *Romeo and Juliet*
2 Peter Fonda
3 Vanessa Redgrave
4 *Last Tango in Paris*
5 *Psycho*
6 Two
7 Melina Mercouri
8 Charlie Chaplin
9 Theda Bara
10 *Revolution*
11 *Mask*
12 Wolfman Jack
13 Australian – she was Annette Kellerman (1888–1975), the film was *Daughter of the Gods*
14 India
15 *Les Enfants du Paradis*
16 Rainer Werner Fassbinder (1946–85)
17 Julie Andrews
18 Abel Gance's (1889–1982)
19 *The Longest Day*
20 *A Clockwork Orange*
21 *Rosemary's Baby*
22 Gina Lollabrigida
23 Harpo
24 Sergei Eisenstein (1898–1948)
25 *A View To A Kill* – the actor is Patrick MacNee

33 · H · The First Time

1 Alcock and Brown in June 1919
2 Henry Hudson (d. 1611)
3 He was the first black actor to win a Best Actor Oscar – for *Lilies of the Field* in 1963
4 Marilyn Monroe (1926–62)
5 Lyndon Johnson (1908–73)
6 Elba
7 Winston Churchill (1874–1965)
8 'Little Boy'
9 Prince Charles
10 The Atlantic – January to July 1969
11 The *Gutenberg Bible*
12 A partridge in a pear tree
13 'Thou shalt have no other gods before me'
14 It was the first feature film to include talking sequences
15 The lightning conductor
16 Queen Elizabeth II
17 Adam Faith
18 Ronald Reagan
19 *Steamboat Willie* (1928)
20 The first link-up in space – it happened on 21 March 1966 when Gemini-8 linked up with the Agena rocket
21 *Midnight Cowboy* (1969)
22 Richard Burton – who married Elizabeth Taylor twice
23 Delaware
24 *The Ten Commandments*
25 *How The West Was Won*

34 · AL · Poet's Corner

1 On the burning deck
2 Emily Dickinson (1830–86)
3 Oscar Wilde (1854–1900)
4 In Westminster Abbey
5 Robert Burns (1759–96)
6 e.e. cummings
7 John Dryden (1631–1700)
8 Alph
9 Gertrude Stein (1874–1946)
10 John Clare (1793–1864)
11 Elizabeth Barrett (1806–61)
12 *Solitude* – by Ella Wheeler Wilcox (1855–1919)
13 Laughing Water
14 Robert Frost (1874–1963)
15 Schiller (1759–1805)
16 W. H. Auden (1907–1973)
17 Skyros – he is Rupert Brooke (1887–1915)
18 John Keats (1795–1821) – he wrote *Ode to a Grecian Urn*
19 'Time's wingèd chariot'
20 Stearns
21 'This Englishwoman'
22 Edward Lear (1812–88)
23 Percy Bysshe Shelley (1792–1822)
24 Samuel Taylor Coleridge (1772–1834)
25 William Blake (1757–1827)

35 · SN · Science for All

1 Nobelium (No) – named after Alfred Nobel (1833–96)
2 Because it's sulphuric acid
3 Salt
4 TNT
5 Sir Isaac Newton (1642–1727)
6 Deoxyribonucleic acid, or DNA
7 Albert Einstein (1899–1955)
8 Acid
9 The first Periodic Table of Elements
10 Du Pont
11 Harder
12 A vacuum
13 The transformation of base metals into gold or silver
14 Mercury
15 Nitrogen
16 Water
17 German silver
18 100 degrees
19 An anaesthetic
20 Red
21 Jean Michel Jarre – his composition was *Oxygene*
22 Diamond – which is mainly carbon
23 *Back to the Future* – Steven Speilberg's film starring Michael J. Fox and Christopher Lloyd
24 Fire
25 Bronze

36 · SL · Tennis

1 Kevin Curren
2 The Swedish royal family
3 a) 55 – he is Bobby Riggs
4 The Federation Cup
5 Le Jeu de Paume – the French name for real or royal tennis, from which tennis evolved. The painting *The Oath of the Tennis Court* is by David
6 Margaret Smith-Court – in the Australian Championships
7 Richard Sears – who won the first seven from 1881 to 1887
8 Andrea Jaeger – when she won the 1981 mixed doubles aged 15 years and 339 days
9 Richard
10 78ft (23.77m)
11 Marianne Simionescu
12 Tim and Tom Gullikson
13 World Championship Tennis
14 He became the first man to achieve the Grand Slam
15 Maureen 'Little Mo' Connolly (USA)
16 *Monsieur Hulot's Holiday* (1952)
17 After the 1924 games
18 In 1973
19 Tracy Austin – aged 16 years and 271 days
20 c) 4 – Czechoslovakian, Bohemia-Moravian, Egyptian and British, as a result of political events and his status as a refugee
21 Yannick Noah
22 John and Tracy Austin
23 The United States Tennis Association
24 Czechoslovakia
25 In 1982

37 · G · The Orient

1 Tibet
2 India
3 The Burma Road
4 Honshu
5 Afghanistan and Pakistan
6 Calcutta
7 *A Passage To India* – the actor is Victor Banerjee
8 China and Japan
9 Shanghai
10 Saigon
11 Indonesia
12 January
13 Samarkand
14 The Caspian Sea
15 Siam (today's Thailand)
16 The Yangtze
17 Israel
18 In Hong Kong harbour – it is the Dragon Boat Race
19 a) The Moluccas – a group of islands in Indonesia, famous for nuts and cloves
20 Hinduism
21 Sikhism
22 The Pakistani rupee
23 The Occident
24 a) north
25 Angkor Wat

38 · E · Making Music

1 By wind passing across the strings
2 The violin
3 Slowly
4 The Moog Synthesizer
5 Jimi Hendrix (1942–70)
6 Stu Sutcliffe
7 Ravi Shankar
8 Jethro Tull
9 Jimi Hendrix (1942–70)
10 Green
11 A violin – the clown is Grock, who was played by Adrien Wettach (1880–1959)
12 Cremona
13 Adolphe Sax (1814–94)
14 The tuba
15 A balalaika
16 An organ scholarship – he is Dudley Moore
17 Ignace Jan Paderewski (1860–1941)
18 David Bowie
19 New York City, with the Metropolitan Opera House, at the Lincoln Center
20 'Happy Birthday'
21 The ukelele – he is George Formby (1905–61)
22 Paul McCartney
23 Japan
24 The oboe
25 Johanna ('Jenny') Maria Lind (1820–87)

39 · H · Law and Order

1 Carmel – the man is Clint Eastwood
2 France
3 Pope John Paul II
4 Judge Roy Bean
5 Pat Garrett
6 Wyatt Earp
7 Sir Robert Peel (1788–1850) – who established the Metropolitan Police Force in 1829
8 King John (1167–1216)
9 Gerald Ford
10 Inspector Clouseau – played by Peter Sellers (1925–80)
11 Andrew Johnson (1808–75)
12 Left-handed
13 The body
14 *Oliver Twist* – the character is Mr Bumble
15 Australia
16 Leaving the scene of an accident
17 Franklin D. Roosevelt (1884–1945)
18 Harrison Ford
19 a) Telly Savalas – who reached number one in the British charts in March 1975
20 Garry Gilmore's
21 The second
22 The UK – the territory is Gibraltar
23 Murphy's Law
24 From Ur – dating from c. 2110 BC
25 A computer made by IBM

40 · AL · Words, Words, Words

1 Gamma
2 Negro
3 English
4 Where are you going
5 Scampo
6 German
7 N
8 A
9 The Rosetta Stone – which provided the key to Egyptian hieroglyphics
10 Aloha
11 From right to left
12 Paprika
13 Amen
14 Newspeak
15 Lightning war
16 German
17 24
18 The siesta
19 The Cambodian alphabet has 72 letters
20 Cha
21 The hoping, or hopeful, one
22 A love letter
23 The Prince of Wales's
24 On the Isle of Man
25 They are kamikaze pilots and kamikaze means 'divine wind'

41 · SN · Numbers and Statistics

1 1000
2 Latitudes 40°–50° South which are characterized by strong winds
3 49
4 a) 12
5 Zero
6 The cubit
7 A contour line
8 The Charge of the Light Brigade – at Balaklava in 1854
9 Two
10 The same bust measurement – they are Jayne Mansfield (1932–67) and Marie Antoinette (1755–93)
11 b) 985ft (300.53m)
12 Three
13 Binary digit
14 Robert Powell
15 That is the temperature at which book paper spontaneously ignites – the plot centres on the destruction of literature in a future society
16 144
17 100 times
18 One foot
19 12
20 c) 1635
21 30 years of marriage
22 Absolute zero
23 MM
24 20
25 24 – the man is Gene Pitney

42 · SL · Champions

1 Bob Champion – played by John Hurt in the film
2 A footrace
3 Cassius X – and later to Muhammad Ali
4 John McEnroe
5 Joe Davis (1903–78)
6 Willie Shoemaker
7 The Hockenheim circuit, West Germany – the driver was Jim Clark (1937–68)
8 41
9 c) 750cc
10 Joe Louis
11 The cheetahs
12 Badminton
13 New Zealander
14 Muhammad Ali
15 The French team – they have won it on 12 occasions
16 Mother's Day
17 Yellow
18 His moustache
19 Guillermo Vilas of Argentina
20 Eusebio
21 Downhill skiing
22 Anatoly Karpov
23 Pakistan
24 Sumo wrestling
25 Rodeo

43 · G · Site Seeing

1 The Leaning Tower of Pisa
2 Nairobi
3 Indonesia
4 Prague
5 Rio de Janeiro
6 Athens's
7 The Palace of Versailles
8 Minnesota
9 London's British Museum
10 The running of the bulls
11 St Peter's – Vatican City
12 July 4 1776
13 Intourist
14 Agra
15 Turkey
16 The Hanging Gardens of Babylon
17 The Rialto
18 Brussels
19 British
20 Queen Victoria's husband, Prince Albert (1819–61) – it is the Royal Albert Hall in London
21 Jerusalem
22 Wiltshire – it is Stonehenge, a prehistoric monument
23 The Great Pyramid of Khufu
24 The famous terracotta army of soldiers
25 Tokyo – none of the other Disneyland sites are in capital cities

44 · E · Dance

1 It was written for baby elephants – to be performed in the circus ring
2 Margot Fonteyn
3 *Swan Lake*
4 Shirley MacLaine and Anne Bancroft
5 Dame Ninette de Valois
6 Leslie Caron
7 St Marylebone – London
8 Danish
9 Odile
10 Michael Clarke
11 Carole Lombard (1908–42)
12 The last Waltz – it was used as a dance hall during the war
13 *Fantasia* – the picture shows the feet of the dancing ostriches
14 Vaslav – he is Nijinsky (1888–1950)
15 Juliet Prowse
16 None – it's a solo
17 They write down dances – using special notation systems to keep a record of the steps and moves of a ballet
18 Mata Hari – the stage name of Margarete Zelle (1876–1917), who spied for the Germans during World War I
19 Four
20 Leningrad
21 No one – it has no music
22 Lola Montez (1818–61) – Irish dancer and adventuress
23 Fred Astaire – she is better known as Ginger Rogers
24 Anna Pavlova (1885–1931)
25 $10 million – she is Cyd Charisse

45 · H · When Was It?

1 May – for Sport Aid
2 b) 1860
3 1933
4 1066
5 August – on 6 August 1945, to be precise
6 b) 1969
7 1900 – she is HRH Queen Elizabeth, the Queen Mother
8 c) 1917
9 The Battle of the Boyne was fought
10 1941 – the writer is Virginia Woolf (1882–1941)
11 c) 1960 – the sailor is Sir Francis Chichester (1901–72)
12 Charles Lindbergh (1902–74) – he made the first solo non-stop transatlantic flight
13 The Hudson Bay Company
14 The Montgolfier brothers made their first flight in a hot air balloon
15 1981
16 c) 1979
17 1901
18 a) 1914
19 a) 1963
20 The Domesday Book
21 St Crispin's Day – 25 October
22 Mrs Indira Gandhi was assassinated
23 1924
24 June – from the fifth to the tenth
25 b) 1976

46 · AL · Old Masters

1 J. M. W. Turner (1775–1851)
2 Fresco – painted on walls or ceilings before the plaster is dry
3 Raphael – the day was 6 April
4 64 – he is Rembrandt (1606–69)
5 Four and a half years
6 Crete
7 Sir Joshua Reynolds (1723–92)
8 Peter
9 Giotto (1267–1337)
10 13
11 Botticelli (1445–1510) – the painting is the *Birth of Venus*
12 Belgium
13 Eyebrows
14 Canaletto (1697–1768)
15 Rembrandt (1606–69)
16 St Peter's – Rome
17 Velasquez (1599–1660)
18 Jacques Louis David (1748–1825)
19 John Constable (1776–1837) – it is entitled *The Leaping Horse*
20 Pieter – they were called The Elder (1525–69) and Hell Brueghel (1564–1638)
21 Jan Vermeer (1632–75)
22 Giorgio Vasari (1511–74)
23 Caravaggio (1569–1609)
24 Henry VIII
25 George Stubbs (1724–1806) – the picture shows one of his drawings for *The Anatomy of a Horse*

47 · SN · Land Animals

1 Beat their chests
2 The rattlesnake
3 The tiger
4 Robert the Bruce (1274–1329) – the creature that inspired him was a spider
5 The elephant
6 A beaver
7 Jaguars
8 None of them
9 Testicles
10 The opossum
11 The giant tortoise
12 The camel family – the creature is a llama
13 Four
14 The duckbilled platypus
15 A wolf
16 Rudyard Kipling (1865–1936)
17 'Earth-pig'
18 Slatey grey
19 The antelope family
20 The caribou or reindeer
21 The ears
22 The Abominable Snowman
23 The giraffe
24 Mrs Tiggywinkle
25 The Romans – the creature is an edible dormouse

48 · SL · Gaming and Gambling

1 Chemin de fer
2 The jack of diamonds
3 15
4 Five aces
5 121
6 Nathan Detroit – in the musical *Guys and Dolls*, adapted from Damon Runyan's story by Joseph Mankiewicz and Frank Loesser
7 Poker – he is American president Harry Truman (1884–1972)
8 Atlantic City – New Jersey, with the Resorts International Casino
9 Blackjack or Twenty-One
10 A deck of cards
11 Three of a kind
12 Seven
13 The 'Kalamazoo'
14 Wild Bill Hickock
15 Bingo
16 Thirty-five to one
17 Robert Shaw
18 Five cents
19 A shooter
20 $5000
21 Slot machines
22 Nine, ten and eleven
23 75
24 Baccarat
25 Five

49 · G · Africa

1 Lake Victoria or Victoria Nyanza
2 Zaire
3 The Atlantic
4 Khartoum – capital of Sudan
5 Zanzibar
6 Morocco
7 Alexandria – he wrote *Alexandria Quartet* from 1957–60
8 Sierra Leone ('Lion Mountain ridge')
9 David Livingstone (1813–73)
10 Morocco
11 France
12 C. S. Forester's (1899–1966)
13 Alan Paton
14 Webster's Dictionary
15 The Sudan
16 Third – after Asia and America
17 Madagascar
18 In Libya – at Al Aziziyah on 13 September 1922. It was 136.4 F (58 C)
19 Libya – it was said that he had received money from Libyan sources
20 Ghana
21 Edgar Rice Burroughs (1875–1950)
22 Hippopotamus comes from the Greek meaning 'river horse'
23 Clarence
24 Henry Morton Stanley (1841–1904)
25 Camelopard

50 · E · Blockbusters

1 Francis Ford Coppola
2 *The Seven Year Itch* – the actress is Marilyn Monroe (1926–62)
3 *The Sound of Music*
4 George Lucas
5 Sylvester Stallone
6 Barbra Streisand – the film was *Yentl*
7 Seven – the actor is Roger Moore
8 *The Exorcist*
9 Three – Tamara de Treaux, Pat Bilson and Matthew de Merritt. The character is E.T., from the film of the same name
10 Chewbacca
11 *Zulu*
12 El Cid
13 Gremlins – from the film of the same name
14 *Around The World In 80 Days*
15 *Gandhi* – an estimated 300 000 people turned out for the funeral scene
16 *Giant*
17 *Chances Are*
18 *Lawrence of Arabia* – the picture shows Vivien Leigh and Clark Gable in *Gone With The Wind*
19 *The Man Who Would Be King*
20 Mario Puzo
21 John Williams
22 A brahman bull
23 *Tales of the South Pacific*
24 *Tomorrow Belongs To Me*
25 Clyde

51 · H · Wars and Weapons

1 The Spanish Civil War
2 Egypt's
3 The French Foreign Legion
4 The American Civil War
5 General Douglas MacArthur (1880–1964)
6 The *Enterprise*
7 World War II
8 Hannibal
9 The War of the Roses
10 Camels
11 World War II
12 The Crusades
13 The Vietnam War
14 France and Spain
15 Belgium – the cartoon is of the Duke of Wellington
16 a) 1916 – on 15 September on the River Somme
17 World War I
18 Samuel Colt (1814–62)
19 R2 D2
20 An ancient missile engine for hurling stones etc.
21 11 – the armistice was signed at the 11th hour of the 11th day of the 11th month, of 1918
22 The Hundred Years War between England and France 1337–1453
23 Audie Murphy (1924–71)
24 The Crimean War – the picture is of Florence Nightingale (1820–1910)
25 The Mason-Dixon Line

52 · AL · The Ancients

1 The Gorgons
2 The fox
3 Troy – it is the wooden horse, in which Greek soldiers were hidden. They destroyed the city
4 Twelve
5 Narcissus
6 His right heel
7 Ambrosia
8 Pandora's
9 Virgil (70 BC–19 BC)
10 The Roman civilization
11 Taoism
12 Alexander Pope (1688–1744)
13 Rome – it is Trajan's Column
14 Electra, daughter of Agamemnon
15 Ovid (43 BC–AD 18)
16 By ensuring that her prophecies were not believed
17 Aeschylus (525 BC–456 BC)
18 Poseidon
19 Crete – they are bull-jumping
20 Mycenae
21 b) Doric
22 *Ben Hur*
23 Robert Graves (1895–1986)
24 The death of Alexander the Great
25 Spartacus

53 · SN · Plant Life

1 The cedars of Lebanon
2 The air
3 Water
4 In its leaves
5 The dandelion
6 The opium poppy
7 Kew Gardens in London
8 The orchid
9 From the bark
10 Pulverized tobacco
11 Sequoiah
12 The picture shows a white cabbage, and *Pieris brassicae* is the cabbage white butterfly
13 The mushroom
14 Seeds
15 Genetics
16 Triffids – from *The Day of the Triffids*
17 Yew trees
18 In the USSR
19 Niger – it is 31 miles (50 km) from any other tree
20 George Orwell (Eric Blair) (1903–50)
21 The crocus
22 The rose – she is Bette Midler who starred in the film *The Rose*
23 b) south
24 China
25 The Swedish scientist Carl Linnaeus (1707–78)

54 · SL · Motor Sports

1 Le Mans
2 Volkswagen's – Formula Vee was the first class for cars built round standard one-make components
3 The Isle of Man
4 The Netherlands
5 Memorial Day – 30 May
6 The Bonneville Salt Flats
7 Mario Andretti
8 Formula One
9 Le Mans Start
10 *The Great Race*
11 France – in 1906
12 Belgrade
13 In a Honda
14 Long Beach – California
15 The Pike's Peak hillclimb – first held in 1916
16 The Mini Cooper S
17 Ettore Bugatti (1882–1967)
18 Ferrari – which has been competing since 1948
19 Tyrrell – the car was the Tyrell Project 34/2, first run in 1976
20 Jackie Stewart in 1979
21 Lotus
22 Jack Brabham – who won the title driving his Repco-Brabham in 1966
23 Belgian
24 Graham Hill (1929–75)
25 Moto-Cross (also known as scrambling)

55 · G · Highspots

1 James Hilton
2 They are the first to have stood on the peak of the world's highest mountain, Mount Everest – they are Tenzing Norgay and Edmund Hillary
3 Aconcagua – Argentina. The highest peak in the Andes at 22 834ft (6 960m)
4 Mount McKinley – the highest mountain in North America at 20 320ft (6 194m)
5 Tanzania – Kilimanjaro is 19 340ft (5 894m) high
6 Mount Ararat – in Turkey. The vessel is Noah's Ark
7 Mount Olympus
8 Bolivia – the city is La Paz (its *de facto* capital)
9 Mount Sinai
10 Island of Martinique
11 Rio de Janeiro in Brazil
12 Sir George Everest (1790–1866) – sometime Surveyor General of India
13 Austria and Italy
14 Italy
15 The Urals
16 In Canada – the CN Tower in Toronto
17 In Afghanistan – through the Hindu Kush
18 George Washington, after whom Mount Washington in the White Mountains is named
19 Mount Vesuvius
20 Theodore Roosevelt (1858–1919)
21 *The Eiger Sanction*
22 The Sears Tower – in Chicago, Illinois in 1974. The picture shows the Empire State Building in New York
23 John Denver
24 Trafalgar Square – the picture shows Nelson's Column, London
25 Lake Titicaca in South America – 12 506ft (3 811m) above sea level

56 · E · The Wild West

1 Calamity Jane
2 Ty Hardin
3 Tombstone – Arizona
4 Roy Rogers
5 *High Noon* (1952)
6 Louis L'Amour
7 Sean Connery – the movie was *Shalako* (1968), the leading lady Brigitte Bardot
8 Tonto – the Lone Ranger's companion
9 Steve McQueen (1930–80)
10 The Pony Express
11 Chingachgook
12 Marlene Dietrich
13 *Rawhide*
14 John Ford
15 Davy Crockett
16 Calgary
17 Doc
18 Lee Marvin
19 Frank James
20 James Drury
21 William Cody (1846–1917)
22 Robert Redford
23 Burt Bacharach – the song was *Raindrops Keep Falling on My Head* in *Butch Cassidy and the Sundance Kid*
24 Rin Tin Tin
25 *Blazing Saddles*

57 · H · Battles and Rebellions

1 The army of the USSR
2 The Crimean War
3 The Battle of Little Big Horn (1876)
4 Lord Cornwallis (1732–1805) – he surrendered to George Washington (1732–99)
5 *I Wish I Was in Dixieland*
6 Field Marshal Montgomery (1887–1976) and Field Marshal Rommel (1891–1944)
7 Tchaikovsky's *1812 Overture*
8 Fletcher Christian
9 Waterloo
10 China
11 The Sudan – British troops defeated the forces of the Mahdi at the Battle of Atbara in 1898
12 Belgium
13 Kenya
14 Battle of Bosworth Field (1485)
15 Joan of Arc
16 The Winter Palace, Leningrad – during the Bolshevik Revolution (1917)
17 Africa – they landed at Algiers and Casablanca
18 Sunday 7 December 1941
19 Constantinople (today Istanbul) – former capital of the Byzantine empire
20 Battle of Lepanto (1571)
21 General John J. Pershing (1860–1948)
22 Battle of Hastings (1066)
23 The Russian Revolution of 1917 – the man is Lenin (1870–1924)
24 The Battle of the Bulge (1944–5)
25 The Emperor Claudius (10 BC–AD 54)

58 · AL · Men in Print

1 Hans Christian Andersen (1807–75)
2 A French poodle
3 *Tropic of Cancer* and *Tropic of Capricorn*
4 *Animal Farm*
5 Ken Kesey
6 *Steppenwolf*
7 *Oliver's Story*
8 Sir Arthur Conan Doyle (1859–1930) – named his character Sherlock Holmes
9 Vincent van Gogh (1853–90)
10 Alexander Solzhenitsyn
11 *Uncle Remus*
12 *The Guinness Book of Records*
13 *The Two Towers*
14 *The Mystery of Edwin Drood*
15 Tuberculosis
16 Alvin Toffler
17 *Papillon*
18 Edgar Allen Poe's (1809–49)
19 Nevil Shute
20 Jude – from *Jude the Obscure*
21 *Shogun*
22 *The Poseidon* – in *The Poseidon Adventure*
23 *Armageddon*
24 Joseph Conrad (1857–1924)
25 Norman Mailer – the star is Marilyn Monroe (1926–62)

59 · SN · Medicine

1 The mosquito
2 Valium
3 A carcinogen
4 Near-sighted
5 Rabies
6 A cold
7 The moment of conception – demonstrated by a sea-urchin
8 Yeast
9 Welby – in the TV series *Marcus MD*
10 Aspirin
11 Three times a day
12 Polio
13 Morphine
14 He was hanged because of it – he is Dr Crippen (1862–1910), who murdered his wife and escaped to America on board an Atlantic liner, only to be caught because of the newly-installed wireless
15 Hippocrates
16 Hypoxemia, or lack of blood to the brain
17 Richard Chamberlain
18 German measles
19 Leukaemia – the film is *Love Story*
20 The male
21 Influenza
22 Dr Christiaan Barnard
23 Electrocardiogram
24 Motor Neurone Disease – he is actor David Niven (1909–84)
25 Bubonic Plague

60 · SL · Golf

1 Mary Queen of Scots (1542–87)
2 Four and a quarter inches (106 mm)
3 Greg Norman
4 Wood
5 Gary Player
6 Bernhard Langer
7 Three strokes fewer than par for a hole
8 In Japan – the seventh hole on the Sano course, Satsuki GC is 909 yd (831 m) long
9 A three wood
10 The Augusta National Golf Course, Georgia
11 Four
12 1983 – the man is Bob Hope, whose British Classic Golf Tournament was last played in 1983 after accusations of financial mismanagement
13 Nine
14 The match between the universities of Oxford and Cambridge
15 Palm Springs
16 On a mound or pinch of sand
17 Lee Trevino
18 Tom Watson
19 Four inches (102 mm)
20 1979
21 Five
22 Peru – the course is over 14 000 ft (4267 m) above sea level
23 The PGA – the Professional Golfers' Association championship
24 A putt
25 The British Open

61 · G · The Seven Seas

1 Pepi – the film was based on the life of sea captain Geoffrey Thorpe
2 The Marianas Trench – 6.78 miles (10.91kms) deep
3 *Double-Eagle V*
4 The Mediterranean Sea
5 Sir Francis Drake (c. 1540 – 96) – who renamed the ship the *Golden Hind* during his 1577–80 voyage
6 The Arctic Ocean
7 Vitus Bering (1681–1741) – Danish navigator
8 *The Cruel Sea* – by Nicholas Monsarrat
9 The Black Sea
10 Iran
11 a) 80%
12 Bluto
13 Portugal – Henry the Navigator (1394–1460) built an observatory and school of navigation
14 The Atlantic
15 The Caspian Sea – 143 550 miles² (371 800km²)
16 *Sailing* – the singer is Rod Stewart
17 b) 60°S
18 Venice
19 Isambard Kingdom Brunel (1806–59)
20 The Indian Ocean
21 Poseidon
22 The Strait of Gibraltar
23 Sea of Marmara
24 Canada
25 Two hours each – the other watches are each of four hours

62 · E · Rock'n'Roll

1 Iowa – he is Buddy Holly (1936–59)
2 Led Zeppelin
3 Bill Haley and his Comets
4 Aaron
5 Brian Jones
6 Duane Eddy – one of the first rock stars to use an electric guitar
7 The E Street Band – Bruce Springsteen is pictured
8 Queen
9 Phil and Don – Everly, who together formed the Everly Brothers
10 The Crickets
11 Cliff Richard
12 Black – from their hit single *Paint It Black*
13 The Candystore Prophets played the music for the Monkees early hits – the Monkees were a group of actors who did not at first perform their own songs
14 Lefthanded – he is Jimi Hendrix (1942–70)
15 Alice Cooper
16 Eric Clapton
17 Status Quo
18 *Blue Hawaii*
19 Roger Daltrey
20 Herman Hesse (1877–1962) – German poet and novelist
21 *Piper At The Gates of Dawn* – by Pink Floyd. The book was written by Kenneth Grahame (1859–1922)
22 Jerry Lee Lewis
23 Billy Fury
24 Adam and the Ants
25 Teddy – together they formed the Beverley Sisters

63 · H · Heads of State

1 Nicholas Breakspear (Adrian IV) (c.1115–59)
2 Lenin (1870–1924)
3 Austria
4 Gamel Abdel Nasser (1918–70) – President of Egypt
5 Louis XIV (1638–1715)
6 He was killed in a car crash
7 He was his son-in-law
8 Haile Selassie – Emperor of Ethiopia (1930–74)
9 Caesar
10 Hawaii
11 Japan
12 Ludwig II of Bavaria (1845–86)
13 Ethelred II (968–1016) – he was known as 'Unready' because he was never able to foresee events and prepare for them
14 The Black Prince (1330–76)
15 Sir Wilfred Laurier (1841–1919)
16 Jawaharlal Nehru (1889–1964)
17 Grand Master la Vallette – he defended the island against a Turkish seige in 1565 and gave his name to Valetta
18 Augustine, first Archbishop of Canterbury (d.604), later canonized
19 a) third – he is Thomas Jefferson (1743–1826)
20 Lady Jane Grey (1537–54) – Queen of England for nine days in 1553
21 Pop star Elton John's – the future head of state is HRH Prince Charles
22 Queen Anne (1665–1714)
23 French – he was Gregory XI (1329–78)
24 France
25 Sailing – the king was Constantine II

64 · AL · Modern Fiction

1 Mordor
2 Italy
3 Evelyn Waugh (1903–66)
4 Catch-22
5 *1984*
6 *Jonathan Livingstone Seagull*
7 Her novel *The Prime of Miss Jean Brodie*
8 *The Godfather* – the actor is Marlon Brando, photographed in 1947
9 *The Devil's Alternative*
10 Harvard
11 *Of Human Bondage*
12 Irwin Shaw's
13 E. M. Forster (1879–1970)
14 Alice Springs – Australia
15 *Gentlemen Prefer Blondes* –by Anita Loos
16 Slavery
17 *Midnight Cowboy* – Dustin Hoffman played Rico Rizzo
18 L. P. Hartley (1895–1972) – the novel is *The Go-Between*
19 Baron Von Richthofen – the novelist is D. H. Lawrence (1885–1930) who was married to Von Richthofen's cousin
20 Denis Wheatley
21 *The Mirror Crack'd From Side To Side* – from *The Lady of Shalott*. The novel is called *The Mirror Crack'd*
22 Amis – the father is Kingsley, the son Martin
23 Adrian Mole – who is the creation of Sue Townsend
24 *The French Lieutenant's Woman*
25 Jeffrey Archer – author of such books as *Cain and Abel* and also Deputy Chairman of the Conservative Party

65 · SN · Space

1 Stanley Kubrick
2 Edwin 'Buzz' Aldrin Jr
3 Project Mercury
4 Star Wars – SDI stands for Strategic Defence Initiative
5 7 – the programme is *Blake's Seven*
6 Venus
7 Alan B. Shepard – who played the first game of golf on the moon in 1971
8 A black hole
9 Two
10 France
11 Czech – he was Vladimir Remek who flew in Soyuz 28 in March 1978
12 Britain
13 Apollo 8 – made the first orbit of the moon in 1968
14 Eagle
15 Three
16 Valentina Tereshkova – who flew in Vostok 6 in June 1963
17 Apollo 1
18 Vulcan – he is Mr Spock, half-human and half-Vulcan, from *Star Trek*
19 H. G. Wells (1866–1946)
20 Werner von Braun (1912–77)
21 Edward H. White II in Gemini 4, in June 1965
22 None
23 Australia
24 Mars
25 Leika – she was launched into space in 1957 aboard Sputnik II

66 · SL · Cheers!

1 Amoroso
2 Champagne and stout – Guinness for preference
3 White
4 A margarita
5 The Bloody Mary
6 Dry
7 Gin
8 Coffee beans
9 Green
10 Celery
11 A triangle
12 Tawny
13 Table wine
14 Salt, tequila, lemon
15 Champagne
16 Benedictine and brandy
17 Grand Marnier
18 Right
19 Aquavit
20 The martini
21 Indian clubs – used for exercise
22 Portugal
23 Hungary
24 Champagne – he is Dom Perignon, inventor of the method Champagnoise
25 Shaken but not stirred

67 · G · World Symbols

1 KLM – the national airline of the Netherlands
2 Blue
3 Tokyo – Narita Airport
4 Eleven
5 The edelweiss
6 The scarlet pimpernel
7 Nepal
8 Kentucky
9 The skull and crossbones
10 Christianity
11 The crescent shape of the new moon
12 The Plimsoll Mark
13 Green
14 Canada – it is the beaver
15 CD
16 Gold
17 The greyhound
18 The leek
19 National Aeronautics and Space Agency
20 Denmark's
21 The cock
22 Athene – goddess of wisdom
23 Cyprus
24 The Sunshine State
25 Yin and Yang

68 · E · Cartoon Time

1 Tom and Jerry
2 Penguins
3 *The Lady and the Tramp*
4 Jellystone National Park
5 Deputy Dawg
6 A basinful of champagne
7 Bugs Bunny
8 *Fantasia*
9 Swee'pea
10 *The Jungle Book*
11 *Bambi*
12 *Gulliver's Travels*
13 *The Fox and the Hound* – which cost $10 million
14 Goofy
15 Donald Duck's
16 Baloo the Bear
17 *One Hundred and One Dalmations* – she is Cruella de Vil
18 Speedy Gonzales
19 United Productions of America, creators of Mr Magoo, Gerald McBoing and Pete Hothead
20 *Snow White and the Seven Dwarfs*
21 *Top Cat*
22 Sylvester
23 Walt Disney used his own voice
24 Woody Woodpecker
25 Pinocchio – his nose grows longer

69 · H · Ancient Worlds

1 Alexander the Great (356–323 BC)
2 The Persians
3 The Emperor Claudius (10 BC–AD 54)
4 Hannibal (247–182 BC) – Carthaginian soldier
5 The lighthouse on the island of Pharos, built in 270 BC but destroyed by earthquakes
6 Greek – she is Cleopatra (69–30 BC)
7 The construction of the Great Wall of China – completed c.200 BC
8 Three
9 Vesuvius
10 Horse racing
11 c) 45 000 – it is the Coliseum in Rome, built cAD 75–80
12 Plato (c.427–c.347 BC)
13 Pontius Pilate
14 Babel
15 Gnaeus Pompey (106–48 BC)
16 Socrates (before 469–399 BC)
17 Aqueducts
18 Constantine (c.274–337)
19 After – between AD 800 and 900
20 Knossos – on Crete
21 January – named after Janus who presides over the 'entrance' to the year
22 Londinium
23 Britain – he was elected consul in AD 77 and followed as governor of Britain
24 Tigris and Euphrates – Mesopotamia is the Greek for 'between the rivers'
25 Athens – it is the Parthenon, built in 447–32 BC on the Acropolis

70 · AL · Settings

1 The Louvre
2 In his bathroom – it is the *Mona Lisa* by Leonardo da Vinci (1452–1519)
3 In Florence – Italy
4 Never Never Land
5 Twelve Oaks
6 Jay Gatsby
7 Two
8 *Sleuth*
9 Spain
10 The Floss – in *The Mill on the Floss* by George Eliot (1819–80)
11 Bonn
12 Australia
13 Lancashire – the artist is L. S. Lowry (1887–1976)
14 Montmartre
15 Earth
16 Mars
17 Michelangelo (1475–1564)
18 *Twelfth Night*
19 *Goodbye Columbus*
20 In Paris and London
21 The world's largest painting
22 In Malibu – California
23 Florence – from the film of E. M. Forster's novel *A Room with a View*
24 Flatford Mill – painted by John Constable (1776–1837)
25 Upon Westminster Bridge

71 · SN · Flight

1 London
2 Amelia Earhart (1898–1937)
3 The speed of sound
4 Paris
5 Two
6 W.E. Johns – the air ace is Captain James Bigglesworth, known as Biggles
7 Vertical Take-Off and Landing
8 Orville Wright – whose passenger was killed in a crash in 1908
9 The Soviet Union's Aeroflot
10 Le Bourget, Paris
11 *The Dam Busters*
12 Monaco – the competitions were held for seaplanes
13 The first Flying Doctor Service
14 The autogyro
15 The first London to Paris air race
16 *Flying Down To Rio* (1933)
17 Louis Blériot (1872–1936) – the plane was called *La Berline de Deutsch*
18 The Soviet Union's – the plane was the Tupolev TU-144
19 Howard Hughes himself
20 The Tornado
21 The German airline, then called Deutsche Luft-Hansa, in May 1926
22 Rio de Janeiro, via Dakar in Senegal
23 None
24 *Enola Gay*
25 The French Revolution – the balloonists are the Montgolfier brothers

72 · SL · World Games

1 Roller derby
2 Tungsten
3 Lawn bowls
4 Six
5 Fencing
6 Skydiving
7 Four
8 Skateboarding
9 Surfers
10 Chess
11 Karate
12 The heart
13 The clay pigeon
14 King Dyal – who supports the West Indies
15 Bullfighting
16 Soccer teams
17 Weightlifting
18 A horse race in the rain
19 The Russian invasion of Afghanistan
20 Judo
21 Cyclocross
22 World Boxing Council
23 Archery
24 The Tour de France
25 Blue

73 · G · Islands

1 Goat Island
2 Melos
3 On the island of St Helena – (where Napoleon Bonaparte died) 1 320 miles (2 120kms) away
4 Mauritius – the bird is the dodo
5 In the pancreas – they are groups of small granular cells that secrete insulin
6 Sicily – it is Mount Etna. The illustration shows its eruption in 1669
7 The islands of Western Samoa – where Robert Louis Stevenson (1850–94) died on the island of Upolu
8 The tropic of Cancer
9 99 years
10 Hispaniola
11 Berne – in Switzerland
12 Great Britain
13 The Falkland Islands
14 The flag of the United Kingdom
15 The Hebrides Overture – the view is of Fingal's Cave
16 Paul Gaughin (1848–1903)
17 Jamaica – he is Sir Noel Coward (1899–1973)
18 Devil's Island
19 Robinson Crusoe – created by Daniel Defoe
20 The flag of Chile
21 The Islands of Hawaii
22 The actress Lily Langtry – who was born in Jersey, one of the British Channel Islands
23 Faeroe Islands
24 The Duke of Windsor (1894–1972) – formerly Edward VIII, who was posted to the Bahamas after abdicating and marrying Mrs Simpson
25 Cyprus

74 · E · Pop Music

1 The Drifters
2 The Wailers – he is Bob Marley (1945–81)
3 Culture Club – he is lead singer Boy George
4 Paul McCartney
5 Ringo Starr
6 Jim Morrison (1943–71)
7 Cass Elliot (1943–77)
8 *Barbarella* – which featured a villain called Duran Duran, after whom the group named themselves
9 Nico
10 Bob Dylan
11 Dire Straits – he is Mark Knopfler
12 A billion – Alice Cooper's 1973 album was titled *Billion Dollar Babies*
13 Phil Spector
14 Peter Tork
15 *Play Misty for Me*
16 The Beach Boys
17 A Granny Smith
18 Waterloo – *Waterloo* was the title of Abba's Eurovision Song Contest hit, which links it with Waterloo Station and the site of the Battle of Waterloo
19 John Denver
20 Stewart Copeland
21 *Thriller* – by Michael Jackson, which had sold 35 million copies by May 1985
22 Chubby Checker – in 1960 (America) and 1962 (UK)
23 Warren Beatty
24 Motown
25 *My Way*

75 · H · Anniversaries

1 6 January
2 St Nicholas's
3 The signing of the Constitution in 1787
4 A grouse
5 Juliet – in *Romeo and Juliet*
6 4 July – Independence Day
7 Charles II – his birthday and date he returned from exile to London
8 1 March
9 John Keats
10 Hallowe'en
11 Walpurgis Night
12 St Swithin
13 St Andrew's Day – 30 November
14 St Patrick's Day – 17 March
15 1 May
16 31 May 1669
17 July – she was married to Prince Charles on 29 July 1981
18 9 August 1945
19 Henry VIII – the year was 1536 and the three wives were, in chronological order, Catherine of Aragon (1485–1536), Anne Boleyn (1504–36) and Jane Seymour (1509–37)
20 Jimmy Carter – the date is 1 October
21 The storming of the Bastille (1789)
22 Haiti – declared independent on 1 January 1804
23 St Valentine's Day – 14 February
24 Johann Sebastian Bach (1685–1750)
25 100 – both events occurred on 12 April, in 1961 and 1861 respectively

76 · AL · Names and Titles

1 *Richard III*
2 *The Lady Vanishes*
3 George Sand (1804–76)
4 *Gone With the Wind* – by Margaret Mitchell (1900–49)
5 Dorian Gray – in *The Portrait of Dorian Gray*
6 John Lennon's (1940–80)
7 *Penthouse*
8 A steam launch
9 Miss Jean Brodie – in *The Prime of Miss Jean Brodie* by Muriel Spark
10 Cleopatra – in *Antony and Cleopatra*
11 Michelangelo
12 *Pride and Prejudice*
13 Ellery Queen – the pseudonym of authors Frederic Dannay and Manfred B. Lee
14 *Twelfth Night*
15 Aphra Behn (1640–89)
16 Samuel Pepys (1633–1703)
17 Plato
18 Tinkerbell – who appears in *Peter Pan* by J. M. Barrie (1860–1937)
19 *The Inn of the Sixth Happiness*
20 Svengali
21 The Brothers Grimm
22 George Orwell (1903–50)
23 Salvador Dali
24 Bonaparte
25 Groucho Marx's (1890–1977)

77 · SN · Domestic Science

1 Four
2 68 °F
3 20
4 Inventing the flush toilet
5 Paper patterns for dresses
6 Carbon dioxide, CO_2
7 The left
8 Six
9 Napoleon's army
10 Three
11 Salad dressing
12 Japan
13 One calorie
14 A two-bulb electric fire from 1911–12
15 Brewing tea automatically
16 The brassiere
17 Lavatory paper
18 Thomas Alva Edison in 1877
19 Barthélemy Thimmonier (1793–1854) – who invented a sewing machine in 1829
20 Melville R. Bissell
21 *Macbeth*
22 The television – which he invented using a mechanical system in 1925–26
23 Bulb
24 The bull's head opener
25 Walter Hunt

78 · SL · Water Sports

1 New South Wales – on Blowering Dam Lake
2 *Courageous*
3 The English Channel
4 Go
5 Backstroke races
6 Nine – eight oarsmen and one cox
7 c) 20 knots
8 The butterfly – which was separated from the breaststroke
9 Canada
10 Seven
11 The backstroke – he is John F. Kennedy
12 A ketch
13 Water skis
14 Self-contained underwater breathing apparatus
15 Olympic size
16 Ireland
17 Edward Heath – the yacht is *Morning Cloud*
18 The water ski
19 Perth
20 Synchronized swimming
21 A swimming pool
22 A white shark – weighing 2664 lb (1208.38 kg)
23 Clarence 'Buster' Crabbe
24 River Severn in England
25 Rowing – the star is Grace Kelly, who became Princess Grace of Monaco

79 · G · Down Under

1 The Southern Cross
2 Abel Tasman (1603–c.1659)
3 The Ross Dependency
4 Tasmania
5 The Great Barrier Reef
6 *The Sundowners* (1960)
7 Perth
8 Woomera
9 b) 1851
10 Ned Kelly (1855–80) – the picture shows Mick Jagger on television
11 A didgeridoo – it is an Aborigine instrument
12 Wellington is on the North Island
13 Barrie Humphries
14 Darwin
15 Walter Burley Griffin
16 The Nullarbor Plain in the south of Australia
17 Harold Holt
18 The Sydney Harbour Bridge
19 The Eureka Stockade
20 The North Island
21 The emu
22 The kiwi fruit
23 Olivia Newton-John
24 Ayer's Rock
25 Melbourne

80 · E · Stage Hits

1 *1776*
2 *Camelot*
3 *Porgy and Bess*
4 *Kismet*
5 *The Rocky Horror Show*
6 The Royal Shakespeare Company – the show is *Nicholas Nickleby*
7 Diane Keaton
8 *The Little Foxes*, by Lillian Hellman
9 *Grease*
10 *Barnum* – starring Michael Crawford
11 *The Elephant Man*
12 *Hair*
13 He appears as a hologram – the actor is Lord Olivier
14 Joel Grey
15 *Green Grow the Lilacs*
16 *Evita*
17 *Camelot*
18 Mark Twain (1835–1910)
19 *Bye Bye Birdie* – which was centred on Elvis Presley (1935–77)
20 *My Fair Lady*
21 *Becket*
22 Stephen Sondheim
23 George Gershwin (1898–1937) – with *Of Thee I Sing*
24 *Chess* – they are Tim Rice, Benny Andersson and Bjorn Ulvaeus
25 *Godspell*

81 · H · The Common People

1 Slavery
2 Franklin D. Roosevelt (1882–1945)
3 The House of Commons
4 The middle class
5 New York City
6 The Black Death, or Bubonic Plague
7 African slaves
8 Sharpeville
9 Cambodia – now Kampuchea
10 UNICEF
11 William Booth (1829–1912) – who founded the Salvation Army
12 Aaron Copland
13 *A Man For All Seasons*
14 Friedrich Engels (1820–95)
15 New Zealand – in 1893
16 Giuseppe Garibaldi (1807–82)
17 Marks and Spencer
18 *Liberté, Egalité, Fraternité*
19 Montgomery
20 Little Rock High School – Arkansas
21 Richard II (1367–1400) – the Peasants' Revolt took place in 1381
22 The Franco-Prussian War (1870–71)
23 The Commonwealth
24 The Atlantic Charter
25 He couldn't afford the fare – he is Karl Marx (1818–83)

82 · AL · Three Dimensions

1 Auguste Rodin (1840–1917)
2 Florence – in the Accademia
3 Furniture – he wrote *The Cabinet Maker's and Upholsterer's Drawing Book*
4 Peter Pan
5 Her arms
6 Mahogany
7 His *Pietà* – which was damaged in an attack
8 Gustave Eiffel (1832–1923) – the Eiffel Tower
9 Henry Moore – English sculptor
10 Le Corbusier (1887–1965)
11 The entrances to some metro stations
12 Sir Christopher Wren (1632–1723)
13 Benvenuto Cellini (1500–71)
14 Landscapes and gardens – his real name was Lancelot Brown (1716–83)
15 Sir Terence Conran
16 The Statue of Liberty – presented to America by the French in 1884
17 Sir Alec Issigonis – the car is the Mini, introduced in 1959
18 Brighton – it is the Brighton Pavilion, built in 1817 for the Prince Regent (later George IV)
19 Donatello (c.1386–1466)
20 Inigo Jones (1573–1652)
21 Bicycle handlebars
22 Sir Edwin Landseer (1802–73)
23 Charlton Heston
24 Wedgwood
25 The Bauhaus – a school of design founded by Walter Gropius in Germany, 1919

83 · SN · Motor Transport

1 The Stanley Steamer
2 The 'Tin Lizzie'
3 12 volts
4 Saturday
5 New York and Paris
6 Switzerland
7 The parking meter
8 Eddie Cochran
9 Henry Ford
10 *Goldfinger* – No. 24 is of course Sean Connery, alias James Bond
11 Lincoln Continental Executive
12 Mexico City
13 The Mini
14 Ferdinand Porsche (1875–1951)
15 A red flag
16 c) carburettor
17 *Genevieve* – which appeared in the movie of the same name
18 Lord Nuffield
19 Tread
20 Turin – FIAT stands for 'Fabbrica Italiana Automobili Torino'
21 Red – they changed to black during 1933
22 By an electric motor – the feat was achieved in 1899
23 Seat belts
24 Sir Clive Sinclair – inventor of the Sinclair C5
25 Isadora Duncan (1878–1927)

84 · SL · All American Sports

1 Horse racing
2 Judge Kenesaw Mountain Landis (1866–1944)
3 Eight seconds
4 Seven feet (2.13 m) tall
5 The Orange Bowl
6 Teddy Kennedy
7 Cricket and rounders – the game is baseball
8 The Boston Celtics
9 Tigers
10 The American League
11 Babe Ruth's
12 Arizona – the sport is rodeo
13 The centre
14 The Los Angeles Rams
15 Thurman Munson
16 The strike zone
17 Milwaukee's
18 Baseball
19 The Rose Bowl – played at Pasadena, California
20 Babe Ruth
21 Lacrosse
22 *The Winning Team*
23 The catcher's
24 A quarter of a mile (402.3 m) – they are drag racers
25 Canada's

85 · G · Farm Facts

1 Rhubarb and asparagus
2 Rice
3 The avocado
4 Truffles – a form of edible fungus
5 Wheat
6 The pea
7 Corn
8 Molasses
9 Cabbage
10 Beetroot
11 Green
12 Viticulture – the growing of grapes
13 The cabbage
14 Milk
15 Australia
16 Potatoes
17 Hops
18 Pink
19 He was a shepherd
20 The Archers
21 Tasmania
22 Eva Gabor
23 North Dakota
24 The USA – it's Clearwater Rice Inc., at Clearbrook, Minnesota
25 a) The sheep

86 · E · The Entertainers

1 Daniel Massey
2 Lenny Bruce's (1926–66)
3 Tom Jones
4 Schnozzle – he is Jimmy Durante (1893–1980)
5 Frank Sinatra
6 John Osborne
7 Sammy Davis Jr.
8 Coco the Clown
9 Will Rogers (1879–1935) – American comedian
10 Liverpool's Cavern Club – famous because The Beatles had played there in their early days
11 George Burns
12 Jim Henson – inventor of The Muppets
13 Kenny Everett
14 Fanny Brice (1891–1951)
15 The Marx Brothers
16 His violin
17 Bob Hope
18 Joan Rivers
19 Mae West (1893–1980)
20 Eddie Cantor (1892–1964)
21 The cowardly lion
22 1977 – he is Elvis Presley
23 George Jessel (1898–1981)
24 Victor Borge
25 Judy Carne

87 · H · Political Animals

1 John F. Kennedy (1917–63)
2 Sir Winston Churchill (1874–1965)
3 Jan Christian Smuts (1870–1950)
4 Manila, in the Philippines
5 James Monroe (1758–1831) – fifth American president. The capital is Monrovia
6 Adolf Hitler (1889–1945)
7 Theology
8 Abraham Lincoln (1809–65)
9 Napoleon Bonaparte (1769–1821) – the building is the Hôtel des Invalides
10 A Boeing 707
11 Niccolo Machiavelli's (1469–1527)
12 Henry Kissinger
13 Mexico
14 Simon Wiesenthal
15 Kenya
16 The *Queen Elizabeth II*
17 c) Ronald Reagan – who appears as a Nazi in *Desperate Journey*
18 The helicopter – he is Michael Heseltine, who resigned over the Westland affair
19 Nikita Khruschev (1894–1971)
20 Prince Otto von Bismarck (1815–98)
21 Gamel Abdel Nasser (1918–70)
22 He established the 49th parallel as the US-Canadian border
23 General Mohammad Zia ul-Haq
24 39
25 On his chin

88 · AL · Kids' Stuff

1 Tin Tin
2 Jack
3 100 years
4 A cat
5 Gotham City
6 Little Boy Blue
7 Marmalade sandwiches – he is Paddington Bear, created by Michael Bond
8 Giant Grumbo
9 A.A. Milne (1882–1956)
10 Ratty
11 University mathematics teacher – he is better known as Lewis Carroll (1832–98), author of *Alice in Wonderland*
12 A rose
13 West Germany
14 Darling
15 Willie Wonka – from *Charlie and the Chocolate Factory*
16 'A beautiful pea-green boat'
17 C.S. Lewis (1898–1963)
18 The Dormouse
19 Bashful
20 Bounce
21 Arthur Ransome (1884–1967)
22 P.L. Travers
23 *Cinderella*
24 Curds and whey
25 Shere Khan – the tiger

89 · SN · Ships

1 The *Queen Mary*
2 Three dots, three dashes, three dots in the Morse code devised by Samuel Morse (1791–1872)
3 Two fathoms, or 12 feet (3.6m) – it was the call of Mississippi pilots who sounded the river for shallow water
4 One
5 32
6 The *Calypso* – the scientist is Jacques Cousteau
7 The *Marie Celeste*
8 Green
9 The *Andrea Doria*
10 The *Bismarck*
11 The magnetic north
12 A son of a gun
13 The *Santa Maria*
14 The *Fram*
15 Humphrey Bogart (1899–1957) – the movie is *The Caine Mutiny* (1954)
16 a) 12lbs (5kg)
17 A rope supporting a mast or yard
18 She completed the first undersea round-the-world voyage
19 The *Turbinia*
20 RMS *Mauretania*
21 The intelligence ship *Pueblo* – captured by North Korea in 1968
22 Israeli – the destroyer *Eilat* was sunk by Egyptian fired missiles in October 1967
23 The Yangtze River
24 The *Mary Rose*
25 The Battle of Lepanto in 1571

90 · SL · Games

1 Whist
2 Blindman's buff
3 The Pluto Platter – better known as the Frisbee
4 25
5 50
6 The nine of hearts
7 28
8 Two
9 Five
10 Draughts, or checkers
11 25 points
12 Black and white
13 Rubik's Cube
14 A video game
15 Black
16 Tick-tack-toe
17 Three
18 Stones
19 The Philippines – it is the yoyo
20 The kaleidoscope
21 Sounds like
22 Mah-jong
23 Stage and Screen
24 *Risk's*
25 Right

91 · G · Organizations

1 Organization of African Unity
2 By banging his shoe on the table – he is Nikita Khrushchev (1894–1971)
3 Norwegian – Trygve Lie (1896–1968)
4 Organization of American States
5 c) 1949
6 Red Crescent
7 Paris
8 Donald Duck
9 T.H.R.U.S.H. – the picture shows David McCallum in *The Man From U.N.C.L.E.*
10 Australia, New Zealand and the USA
11 The Hague – Netherlands
12 Mexico – he is Fidel Castro
13 U Thant (1909–74)
14 France
15 Ecuador and Venezuela
16 The Netherlands's
17 Pope John XXIII
18 Rome – FAO stands for Food and Agricultural Organization
19 Vatican City (Holy See)
20 The Duke of Edinburgh
21 World Council of Churches
22 Philadelphia
23 The United Kingdom
24 Peace
25 Robert Baden-Powell (1857–1941) – the organization is the Boy Scouts

92 · E · Television

1 David Carradine
2 Kristin Shepard – the picture shows J.R., played by Larry Hagman in *Dallas*
3 Quentin Crisp's – the actor was John Hurt
4 St Elsewhere – from the TV show *St Elsewhere*
5 Michael Praed – who left *Robin of Sherwood* to join *Dynasty*
6 *Monty Python's Flying Circus*
7 Jack Lord
8 *Dempsey and Makepeace* – they are Glynis Barber and Michael Brandon
9 *Till Death Us Do Part*
10 K9
11 Hot Lips – the character is better known as Margaret Houlihan, played by Loretta Swit
12 Henry Winkler – shown as The Fonz in *Happy Days*
13 *The Phil Silvers Show*
14 *Bewitched*
15 Terry McCann and Arthur Daley – played by Dennis Waterman and George Cole
16 Dodge City
17 Five years
18 Derek Jacobi
19 *The Hitch Hiker's Guide to the Galaxy*
20 Lurch
21 Theo – the picture shows Telly Savalas, star of *Kojak*
22 Kermit
23 Lynda Carter – star of *Wonderwoman*
24 Mia Farrow
25 Herbert Lom

93 · H · Third World

1 Yugoslavian – she is Mother Teresa
2 Henry Morton Stanley (1841–1904)
3 Idi Amin
4 c) 1949
5 China
6 Mick Jagger
7 Mali
8 Gamal Abdel Nasser (1918–70)
9 Cuba
10 Salvador Allende (1908–73)
11 Jawaharlal Nehru (1889–1964)
12 The Zulus
13 A football match
14 Bangladesh
15 Saudi Arabia
16 Cambodia, or Kampuchea
17 The Dalai Lama's
18 Haiti – he is Baby Doc, alias Jean-Claude Duvalier, former president-for-life
19 Harold Macmillan
20 Paraguay
21 *The Dogs of War*
22 Tonga – he is King Taufa'ahau
23 Mozambique
24 La Réunion
25 Senegal

94 · AL · American Art and Architecture

1 Maine
2 Frank Lloyd Wright (1869–1959)
3 The Eskimos
4 a) The Hudson – Hudson River School
5 Mobiles
6 Samuel F.B. Morse (1791–1872)
7 Thomas Eakins (1844–1916)
8 Paul Revere (1735–1818)
9 Charles D. Gibson (1867–1944) – creator of the Gibson Girl
10 John Singer Sargent (1856–1925)
11 James McNeill Whistler (1834–1903)
12 Louis Comfort Tiffany (1848–1933)
13 Jackson Pollock (1912–56)
14 R. Buckminster-Fuller
15 Mount Rushmore National Memorial
16 Iowa
17 The Incas
18 Andy Warhol
19 American Primitive
20 Frederic Remington (1861–1909)
21 Anna Mary
22 Handball – in *Handball*
23 Man Ray (1890–1976) – a 'rayograph' is a picture made by placing an object against light sensitive paper
24 Mary Cassatt (1844–1926)
25 Judy Chicago – whose work *The Dinner Party* celebrates women's struggles and achievements

95 · SN · Water Life

1 Ten
2 Tarka
3 Ivory
4 The shark's
5 A dolphin
6 Herring
7 The *Nautilus* – from *20 000 Leagues Under The Sea* by Jules Verne
8 Amity – the film is *Jaws*
9 The turtle – the album is *The Dream of the Blue Turtles*, and the artist is Sting
10 Mussels stewed with butter, white wine and shallots
11 A salmon
12 The crocodile
13 c) cartilage
14 A lobster
15 A jelly-fish
16 Three
17 Hergé
18 Plankton
19 The Russian sturgeon – valued for its caviare (roe)
20 The sardine
21 A calf
22 The ghavial or gavial – found in the rivers of India and Burma
23 Iceland
24 The coelacanth
25 By shooting a jet of water from the surface and knocking insects into the water

96 · SL · The Olympics

1 The women's marathon
2 Jock straps
3 Four – Winter and Summer Games in 1940 and 1944
4 Nikon
5 Baron Pierre de Coubertin (1863–1939)
6 Five continents
7 Longer – the marathon is 26 miles 385 yds (42.195 km)
8 Japan
9 West Berlin
10 South Africa
11 Paavo Nurmi (1897–1973)
12 Never
13 Coca Cola
14 One
15 Super heavyweight
16 France – in 1924
17 Sonja Henie (1910–69)
18 One
19 1984
20 Helsinki
21 Mick Jagger
22 Maple trees
23 Boxing – he is Errol Flynn
24 Princess Anne
25 Misha the bear

97 · G · Money Matters

1 Zurich
2 Life insurance
3 The dinar
4 Greece
5 The Louisiana Purchase from France in 1803
6 Japan's
7 Brazil
8 Guatemala's quetzal
9 From Spain – where the coins were stamped with an 8 to indicate the value of 8 reals
10 Zero
11 Japan
12 *Money, Money, Money* – by Abba
13 United Arab Emirates
14 Kentucky
15 Argentina
16 China, in AD 910
17 Jean Paul Getty (1892–1976)
18 Venezuela
19 Hungary
20 The estate of Howard Hughes (1906–76)
21 The Incas – who filled a hall for Francisco Pizarro with gold and silver in return for Atahualpa
22 *Cabaret* – she is Liza Minelli
23 Western Deep Level, Carletonville, South Africa
24 Ghana
25 Love – in the song *Can't Buy Me Love*

98 · E · Plays and Players

1 *The Mousetrap*
2 Sam Shephard
3 Morphine
4 Arthur Miller
5 Harold Pinter's
6 Oscar Wilde (1854–1900)
7 *Who's Afraid of Virginia Woolf*
8 *A Streetcar Named Desire* by Tennessee Williams – the actress was Vivien Leigh (1913–67)
9 *Equus*
10 Pope John Paul II
11 Samuel Beckett – the actress is Billie Whitelaw
12 Brendan Behan (1923–64)
13 *Statements After an Arrest Under the Immorality Act*
14 Godot – in *Waiting for Godot* by Samuel Beckett
15 *The Rivals* – by Richard Brinsley Sheridan (1751–1816)
16 *A Midsummer Night's Dream* – by William Shakespeare
17 Clifford Odets (1906–63)
18 Noh Theatre
19 Alan Ayckbourn
20 Neil Simon
21 The Method school
22 Bobby Watson
23 Antonio Salieri (1750–1825)
24 Noël Coward (1899–1973)
25 Hamlet – the actor is Sir John Gielgud

99 · H · Words and Ideas

1 Islam
2 Martin Luther King Jr. (1929–68)
3 In Mecca
4 Existentialism – the couple are Jean-Paul Sartre (1905–80) and Simone de Beauvoir (1908–85)
5 Seven
6 The Netherlands
7 Harry S. Truman (1884–1972)
8 Karl Marx (1818–83)
9 Mao Tse-tung (1893–1976)
10 Mormonism
11 Eat meat on a Friday
12 Adam Smith (1723–90)
13 Ludwig Wittgenstein (1889–1951)
14 Héloïse
15 'That's one small step for (a) man, one giant leap for mankind – first reported without the word 'a'
16 a) Confucius (551–479 BC)
17 The fear of the Lord
18 Roman Catholicism
19 The River Ganges
20 Réné Descartes (1596–1650)
21 Russia
22 John Paul I (1912–78)
23 Diogenes of Sinope (c.412–c.325 BC)
24 Thomas More (1478–1535)
25 Germaine Greer

100 · AL · The Classics

1 Sancho Panza
2 Cyrano de Bergerac
3 Esmerelda – in *The Hunchback of Notre Dame* by Victor Hugo (1802–85)
4 Emma
5 The Roman Empire – in *The Decline and Fall of the Roman Empire*
6 *Good Wives*
7 'Yo ho ho and a bottle of rum'
8 *Wuthering Heights*
9 In prison, in Bedford
10 Count Alexis Vronsky
11 Tobias Smollett (1721–71)
12 Donwell Abbey
13 *Far From The Madding Crowd*
14 Sir Walter Scott (1771–1832)
15 Alice Liddell (1852–1934) – in *Alice's Adventures in Wonderland* and *Through the Looking Glass* by Lewis Carroll
16 Mary Shelley (1797–1851) – in *Frankenstein*
17 Mrs Gaskell (1810–65)
18 *The Red Badge of Courage*
19 *Germinal*
20 *The White Peacock*, published in 1911
21 *Candide*
22 The Concord and Merrimac Rivers
23 Ivan Turgenev (1818–83)
24 Six
25 *Ulysses*

101 · SN · Astronomy

1 Jupiter's
2 Halley's comet
3 Aquarius
4 The Milky Way
5 Nicolas Copernicus (1473–1543)
6 Mercury
7 The moon
8 7 minutes 40 seconds
9 The corona
10 Venus
11 Tycho Brahe (1546–1601)
12 The Bonzo Dog Dooh-Da Band
13 The sun
14 a) Pluto
15 The Egyptians – he is Ra
16 One sixth
17 Three
18 David Bowie
19 Saturn
20 Sirius
21 Mars
22 The sun
23 Galileo Galilei (1564–1642) – he was forced to renounce his belief that the Earth revolved around the Sun by the Inquisition
24 Venus
25 Saturn

102 · SL · Food, Glorious Food

1 Water
2 Breadfruit trees
3 Sesame seed
4 The ewe (sheep)
5 Vichyssoise
6 Twice – 'biscuit' comes from the French *bis cuit* meaning twice cooked
7 Marco Polo – he brought pasta from China in the Middle Ages
8 Oliver – in *Oliver Twist*
9 c) 32 times
10 Honey
11 Clarence Birdseye (1886–1956)
12 a) Roast beef with 70 calories per ounce – roast veal has 65 and roast chicken 55
13 On the plains of North America – it is Jerusalem artichoke. It s partner is a globe artichoke
14 A tablespoon
15 Dried and salted fish – usually the bummalo
16 The herring family
17 Saffron
18 Bread sticks
19 A bouquet garni
20 Stuffed
21 Charles de Gaulle (1890–1970)
22 The pig – it is raw smoked ham served finely sliced
23 Julia Child
24 Music
25 Corn Flakes

103 · G · Where in the World

1 In Italy
2 Cape Cod
3 The Canary Islands
4 China
5 The Brandenburg Gate
6 The equator
7 Spain – in Granada
8 Utah
9 The Kimono
10 The Panama Canal
11 Belgium
12 Venice – it is the winged lion
13 Lebanon
14 The Nile
15 A cockney
16 Hong Kong
17 In Paris – in the film *Last Tango in Paris*
18 Stockholm
19 The Tower of London – they are Yeomen Warders
20 The Ukraine
21 In Philadelphia
22 Shah Jehan (1592–1666) – it is the Taj Mahal, built as a tomb for his favourite wife
23 Nigeria's
24 Grenada
25 Ethiopia's – the picture shows Bob Geldof founder of Band Aid and Live Aid

104 · E · Cops and Robbers

1 Six
2 The Sex Pistols – Ronald Biggs is one of the Great Train Robbers
3 *In the Heat of the Night*
4 Five
5 A guillotine
6 The French Connection
7 Captain Frank Furillo
8 They are brothers – they are Telly and George Savalas
9 Broderick Crawford
10 *Serpico* – the story was based on the true story of Frank Serpico
11 A diamond
12 *The Streets of San Francisco*
13 *Naked City*
14 *Police Woman* – the actress is Angie Dickinson
15 Officer Krupke
16 Dick Turpin
17 The Keystone Kops
18 Glenn Ford
19 Roger Daltrey
20 Jules
21 Adam Ant – who had a hit with *Stand and Deliver* in May 1981
22 Starsky
23 Chicago's
24 Sherlock Holmes
25 *Little Caesar* – the actor is Edward G. Robinson (1893–1973)

105 · H · World War II

1 American GI's in Britain
2 Spitfires
3 The attack on Pearl Harbor
4 Italy
5 Gestapo
6 Adolf Hitler
7 Japan and the USA
8 Operation Barbarossa
9 Noël Coward – the picture shows Admiral Earl Louis Mountbatten of Burma (1900–74)
10 Chunking
11 The USSR
12 Italy
13 The Channel Islands
14 HRH Queen Elizabeth, the Queen Mother – after Buckingham Palace was bombed
15 1940 – on 10 May
16 In Normandy
17 A siren suit
18 Benito Mussolini (1883–1945)
19 Joseph P. Kennedy (1888–1969)
20 Vidkun Quisling (1887–1945)
21 Rudolf Hess
22 Egypt
23 The Utility Mark – which was stamped on goods from 1942 to signify a certain standard of design and quality
24 Operation Overlord
25 New Guinea

106 · AL · Shakespeare

1 Verona
2 Cole Porter (1893–1964) – the show was *Kiss Me Kate*
3 *Hamlet* – she is Agatha Christie (1891–1976)
4 Shylock
5 St George – the day is 23 April
6 A type of wine – generally white wines imported from Spain and the Canaries. Some were like sherry
7 He is killed by a bear
8 Sebastian
9 Akira Kurosawa
10 Miranda – in *The Tempest*
11 David Garrick (1717–79)
12 Puck
13 Henry Wrothesley, 3rd Earl of Southampton (1573–1624) – his patron
14 Duncan – King of Scotland
15 The Trojan War
16 Julius Caesar
17 HRH Prince Charles – who played Macbeth as a boy at Gordonstoun School
18 Richard Duke of Gloucester – later Richard III
19 *Henry V*, Act III scene 4
20 Hamnet
21 'my second best bed . . .'
22 *Romeo and Juliet* – the film is *West Side Story*
23 Beatrice
24 Egypt
25 The Forest of Arden

107 · SN · Railways

1 Works of art plundered by the Nazis
2 Mount Fuji in Japan
3 Casey Jones
4 Switzerland
5 France – TGV stands for Train de Grande Vitesse
6 In Australia – it runs for 297 miles (478 kms) across the Nullabor Plain
7 In Utah, at Promontory
8 The B.A.R.T. – Bay Area Rapid Transit System
9 He received the first actual golden disc on that date – he is Glen Miller (1904–44)
10 Mark Twain – the story was *Punch, Brothers, Punch*
11 J.M.W. Turner (1775–1851)
12 London, England
13 Colonel Nicholson – played by Alec Guinness
14 Moscow
15 Andrew Lloyd Webber – the musical is *Starlight Express*
16 At the rear – where it is a conductor's van
17 His was the first recorded fatality after a railway accident in 1830
18 The River Tay
19 Grand Central Station, New York City
20 Baltimore and Ohio
21 Rome's
22 A form of rail fastening
23 *Brief Encounter* – starring Celia Johnson and Trevor Howard, made in 1945
24 It's the longest in the world
25 Mr Norris – the novel is entitled *Mr Norris Changes Trains*

108 · SL · Sporting Greats – The Women

1 Vera Caslavska
2 Martina Navratilova
3 In Brazil
4 Hazel Wightman (née Hotchkiss) (1886–1974)
5 HRH Princess Anne
6 Water skiing
7 400 metres
8 Nadia Comaneci of Rumania – in 1976
9 Dawn Fraser of Australia
10 Lucinda Green (née Prior-Palmer)
11 Ice pairs
12 Billy Jean King
13 Esther Williams
14 The mile – she is Mary Decker-Slaney
15 Olga Korbut
16 c) 1900 – but only in the tennis and golf competitions
17 Sue Barker, of Britain
18 Dressage (riding)
19 Kathy Whitworth
20 Fanny Blankers-Koen of the Netherlands
21 In 1920
22 Ann Haydan Jones
23 Darts
24 Sonja Henie
25 She became the first woman ever to swim the English Channel

109 · G · Landmarks

1 Easter Island – the origin of the statues remains a mystery
2 The Ginza
3 France and Italy
4 Table Mountain
5 In Amsterdam – the Netherlands
6 In Singapore
7 Turkey – just inland from the Aegean, where it was a port in ancient times
8 Buckingham Palace
9 In Liverpool
10 On the coast of County Antrim, Northern Ireland
11 The Rockies
12 Lisbon – capital of Portugal
13 The Trevi fountain – in Rome
14 In Agra
15 The Champs Elysées
16 1600 Pennsylvania Avenue – it is the White House, home of the American president
17 The Suez (= Zeus) Canal
18 Martha's Vineyard, off the coast of Massachusetts
19 The Empire State Building
20 Red
21 The civilization of the Incas
22 The clock in St Stephen's Tower in the Houses of Parliament – often called Big Ben after the bell of the original name
23 Mississippi River – the Huey P. Long Bridge, at Melairie, Louisiana is 4.35 miles (7 km) long
24 The Spanish Steps
25 Hollywoodland – the site was originally intended for a real-estate development

110 · E · Comic Cuts

1 Snoopy
2 Asterix
3 *A Charlie Brown Christmas*
4 Robin – Batman's assistant
5 Spiderman
6 Krypton – he is Superman
7 Pogo
8 She's his first cousin
9 Huey, Dewey, Louie
10 Wimpy
11 *Yellow Submarine*
12 Sniff
13 Dino
14 Hagar
15 Snowy – the character is Tintin
16 Fritz the Cat
17 Roadrunner
18 Wonder Woman's
19 His spectacles
20 Donald Duck
21 His fiftieth birthday
22 The Penguin
23 Linus
24 Chic Young (1901–73)
25 Captain Marvel

111 · H · Origins

1 The brontosaurus
2 The blue whale
3 Charles Darwin (1809–82)
4 The horse
5 By land bridge from Siberia
6 In Germany – near Dusseldorf, in 1856
7 Palaeontology is the study of extinct animals and plants from fossil remains
8 The brick
9 The Triassic period
10 *One Million Years BC* – she is Raquel Welch
11 The okapi
12 Africa
13 Its 14 000 year old cave paintings
14 In Kenya
15 A mammoth
16 The Iron Age
17 The skull of Piltdown Man
18 Peking man – the Latin means 'the Chinese man of Peking'
19 Barney Rubble
20 Tyrannosaurus Rex – he is Marc Bolan, who died in 1977
21 *The French Lieutenant's Woman* – from the book by John Fowles
22 The supercontinent formed by all the world's landmass before it divided
23 The bat
24 Walt Disney
25 In New Zealand

112 · AL · Origins of English

1 Curfew
2 X
3 Unto – the abbreviation originally referred to the phrase 'I owe unto . . .'
4 Mongoose – more than one are mongooses
5 Son of
6 Books
7 The comma
8 Of
9 E
10 Thomas Bowdler (1754–1825) – he gave the world the word 'bowdlerize', which means to cut or edit a work prudishly
11 Dreamt
12 Z
13 Cleave
14 Rhythms
15 Opera
16 Jehovah
17 Gas
18 O.K.
19 Plural
20 Richard Nixon's
21 Absent Without Leave
22 Onomatopoeia – for example, the word *cuckoo* sounds like the bird it refers to
23 *The Rivals* (1775) – in which Mrs Malaprop appears, played here by Geraldine McEwen
24 Zenith
25 A spoonerism – named after Rev. William Archibald Spooner (1844–1930), dean and later warden of New College, Oxford

113 · SN · Signs and Symbols

1 Because
2 Bass clef
3 Carbon monoxide
4 Aries
5 The French Resistance – it is the Cross of Lorraine
6 Saturn
7 The ratio of the circumference to the diameter of a circle
8 Gold – *Aurum* in Latin
9 The Earth
10 Not equal to
11 Taurus
12 Ne represents the gas neon which is used in neon tubes and bulbs
13 Female
14 Pierre and Marie Curie – joint winners of the Nobel prize for Chemistry in 1903. The element is Radium
15 Infinity
16 Calcium
17 The moon's last quarter
18 Less than
19 At; to
20 Male
21 The sun
22 Aquarius
23 Mg
24 Parallel
25 Libra

114 · SL · Ball Games

1 Earthball
2 Pele – real name Edson Arantes do Nascimento of Brazil
3 Pelota, or Jai Alai – the instrument is called a *chistera*
4 The yellow ball
5 The Ashes
6 Forest Hills
7 Four – the game is polo
8 Table tennis's
9 India
10 A softball
11 The Aztecs
12 The golf ball
13 Paddle rackets
14 The right
15 Softball
16 Red
17 Squash
18 Soccer's
19 Three times
20 Break service
21 a) Black
22 Badminton – it is played with a shuttlecock
23 Cliff Thorburn – Canadian snooker player
24 Rugby League has 13 players to Rugby Union's 15
25 Ireland's – the game is hurling

115 · G · Wastes and Wildernesses

1 Botswana
2 The Empty Quarter
3 Great Sandy Desert – with an area of 160 000 miles² (420 000 km²) to the Nubian Desert's 100 000 miles² (260 000 km²)
4 Greenland – it is Godthaab
5 c) 1911
6 Bactrian camel (with two humps)
7 The deserts of Australia, which they explored
8 The west
9 Theodore Roosevelt
10 India and Pakistan
11 A sheep – 'Ovis Poli', or Marco Polo sheep
12 The Andes at 4500 miles (7200 km)
13 Spanish – a member of the 1540 expedition led by Francisco Vazquez de Coronado
14 Chile and Argentina
15 *Nanook of the North*
16 The Tuareg
17 Almost six weeks. He spent forty days in the wilderness.
18 a) ½ – it is roughly half the size of Africa: 11 506 000 miles² (29 800 000 km²) to c.5 500 000 miles² (c.13 600 000 km²)
19 Gary Cooper
20 On Antarctica – the Lambert-Fisher Ice Passage is c.320 miles (515 km) long
21 Great Bear Lake at 12 275 miles² (31 800 000 km²) to Lake Ontario's 7520 miles² (19 500 km²)
22 The Sahara
23 *Zabriskie Point*
24 The Hejaz Railway
25 Alice Springs

116 · E · Words and Music

1 *Things We Said Today*
2 *Oklahoma!*
3 *Your Song*
4 Yellow polka dot bikini
5 *All I Really Want To Do*
6 The fruit of the poor lemon
7 *Aquarius*
8 *Cecilia*
9 That was the day Buddy Holly died
10 *She Loves You* and *All You Need Is Love*
11 *San Francisco*
12 An Island in the Sun – he is Harry Belafonte
13 Through the streets of London
14 Joe DiMaggio
15 Barbara Ann
16 Deborah Kerr – who played Anna
17 Sting – of Police
18 John F. Kennedy (1917–63) – the singer is Frank Sinatra
19 My blue suede shoes
20 'Que sera sera, whatever will be will be' – from the song *Whatever Will Be Will Be*
21 Do wah diddy diddy dum diddy do
22 Lily the Pink – they are *Scaffold*
23 *Hernando's*
24 *Substitute*
25 Sonny Bono – the singer is Cher

117 · H · Heroes and Heroines

1 Lord Byron (1788–1824)
2 Fly solo across the Atlantic – she is Amelia Earhart (1898–1937) who flew from Newfoundland to Burry Point, Wales
3 Amelia Bloomer (1818–94) – who gave her name to an early type of women's trouser
4 Switzerland – William Tell is widely thought to have led a drive for Swiss independence in the Middle Ages
5 Bob Geldof's
6 Electrician – he is Lech Walesa, one of the founders of the Solidarity movement
7 *Much Ado About Nothing*
8 Hatshepsut – 18th Dynasty Egyptian ruler who defied tradition to lead her country
9 Boadicea or Boudicca – queen of the Iceni tribe in the 1st century AD, who led her army against the Romans
10 Martin Luther King Jnr (1929–68) – who was assassinated in Memphis, Tennessee, while on a civil rights mission
11 In China, where he quelled the Taiping rebellion
12 The Unknown Soldier – the picture shows the Arc de Triomphe in Paris
13 Moshe Dayan (1915–81)
14 Prince Charles Edward Stewart (1720–88) – also known as the Young Pretender and Bonny Prince Charlie. He escaped after the Battle of Culloden (1746) disguised as Flora Macdonald's maid
15 Marie Curie (1867–1934) – who discovered radium and died of leukemia after absorbing dangerous doses of it during her experiments
16 Edith Cavell (1865–1915)
17 Captain Lawrence Oates (1880–1912) – who, convinced that his frostbite would handicap the rest of the party in their bid to reach safety, sacrificed his life
18 Malta's – because of their fortitude in the face of heavy bombing
19 The French Resistance
20 Horatio Nelson (1758–1805)
21 Joan of Arc (1412–31)
22 Paul Revere (1735–1818) – hero of the American Revolution
23 Portugal's
24 Pocahontas (1595–1617) – who twice saved the life of Captain John Smith
25 Grace Darling (1815–42) – daughter of William Darling, a lighthouse keeper

118 · AL · Women in Print

1 Pills
2 *Peyton Place*
3 *Gone With The Wind*
4 Yoko Ono
5 Pink – she is Barbara Cartland, romantic novelist
6 *Lace* – the author was Shirley Conran, author of the *Superwoman* books
7 New Zealander
8 Agatha Christie (1891–1976)
9 Alice Walker – the book and film are *The Color Purple*
10 Billie Holliday's
11 *A House is Not a Home*
12 Germaine Greer
13 Maya Angelou's
14 Stevie Smith (1902–71)
15 Agatha Christie (1891–1976)
16 Anne Frank's
17 Edna O'Brien's
18 Shirley MacLaine
19 Mrs Isabella Beeton (1836–65)
20 Elinor Glynn (1864–1943)
21 Daisy Ashford
22 Kathleen Mansfield (1888–1923)
23 Doris Lessing
24 Karen Blixen – the film is *Out of Africa*
25 Ann Jellicoe

119 · SN · Eureka

1 The electric battery – the volt is named after the Count (1745–1827)
2 Zip fastener
3 German – Johann Gutenberg (c. 1400–68) invented it c. 1455. His 42 line Latin Bible is illustrated
4 Locksmith
5 Louis Pasteur (1822–95)
6 St John's – Newfoundland
7 George Stephenson (1781–1848) – inventor of the *Rocket* railway locomotive
8 The monkey wrench
9 The electric razor – first manufactured 18 March 1931
10 Thomas Alva Edison (1847–1931)
11 c) 1953 – by the Dunlop Rubber Company
12 Benjamin Franklin (1706–90)
13 Microscope – a compound convex-concave lens
14 Condensed milk
15 His wife's hand
16 George Mortimer Pullman (1831–97)
17 Machine gun – called the Gatling gun
18 Alexander Graham Bell (1847–1922)
19 Margarine – named after *margarites* by Hippolyte Mège-Mouriez, patented 1869
20 Taking a bath
21 The computer
22 Frozen food
23 Nylon
24 Roulette wheel
25 Charles Macintosh (1766–1843)

120 · SL · Winter Sports

1 Bill Johnson – in 1984 with a new Olympic speed record
2 Skiing
3 St Moritz
4 Swedish
5 Anchorage – Alaska
6 *Help!*
7 It's been touched
8 A ski-bob
9 Women's giant slalom
10 British – he was Squadron Leader Mike Freeman, bobsleigher and flag bearer at the 1972 Winter Olympics
11 Toes
12 Kitzbühel
13 Lake Placid
14 Mount Everest
15 Sierra Nevada
16 Princess Andrew, Duchess of York
17 Grenoble
18 Sapporo – Japan
19 Because it's called the Inferno, the name Dante gave to part of his *Divine Comedy*
20 Maurice Ravel (1875–1937) – they are Jayne Torvill and Christopher Dean
21 b) 610 ft (186 m)
22 The highest on skis – 129.30 mph (208.09 km/h), as opposed to 80 mph (128 km/h) on a toboggan
23 Norwegian
24 Fridtjof Nansen (1861–1930) – Norwegian explorer
25 *The Spy Who Loved Me*